Natoma's
Low Fat
Home~Style Cooking

Published by
Alpha LifeSpan

In view of the complex, individual, and specific nature of health and fitness problems, this book is not intended to replace professional medical advice. The author and publisher expressly disclaim responsibility for any liability, loss or risk, personal or otherwise which is incurred as a consequence, directly or indirectly, of the use and application of any of the contents of this book.

To Ryan and Taylor Gray

Though you are little people now,

Memaw is working very hard,

so you may have a healthy heart!

Love,

Memaw

CREDITS:
Evansville Bindery for their vital role in printing this book
LowFat Connection, Inc. for access to Natoma's materials and company literature
Photo credits:
"Images copyright ©, New Vision Technologies, Inc."
Michael Gray Photography for billboard picture
Buehler's Buy-Low, Village Commons, Evansville for helpful suggestions for local
Evansville shoppers
Glamour Shots, Evansville, for cover photo of Mrs. Natoma Riley
Schmitt Photo Services, Inc.
Evansville Press Newspaper, Evansville for vacation photo on p. 241 and
June 15, 1994 article by Andrea Brown.

DISCLAIMER PAGE

The author and publisher of this book are not physicians and are not licensed to give medical advice. The information in this book has been collected for the convenience of the reader. The fat values for prepared foods are subject to change and might currently vary from listings herein, which are based on research conducted in early 1994.

Such information does not constitute a recommendation or endorsement of any individual, institution or product, nor is it intended as a substitute for personalized consultation with your physician. The authors and publisher disclaim any liability arising directly or indirectly from the use of this book.

Neither the author, Alpha Life Span, nor LowFat Connection (LFC) claim that these recipes are original. "I have taken recipes from many sources and reduced them down to the lowest fats as possible, but maintaining their good taste." (N.R.)

ACKNOWLEDGMENTS

To Sue Essary who has spent endless hours defatting and typing recipes that were shared with LFC for this book. We could not have done it without her help.

To Betty Harker, a new friend who came into my life through the LFC connection. She has helped me more than she will ever know.

To Nancy Tomlinson, an old friend who has shared years of her recipes with me so I could defat and pass them along to you, the reader.

To my daughter Sherri Riley, for her saying, "Say Yes and Weigh Less."

To my father Fred Belcher, my mother Dorothy Belcher and my sister Rebecca Perry, for their assistance in taking some of the everyday routines off my shoulders in the early weeks of this book project.

To Barbara Zwickel, printer and friend, for her going above and beyond the call of a "printer's duty" in making this book possible.

To Michael K. Smith for his help with the computers.

To all the "Fatbusters" of LFC out there who helped in contributing recipes.

To Lynn Shaw, owner of Designer 4 Hair & Tanning Salon, Evansville, Indiana, for allowing me to introduce my program publicly to her people.

Most of all, to Frank, my husband and best friend, for his support and belief in me.

PREFACE

It all started seven years ago when I was having difficulty fitting into my size 22 jeans. I realized I had to get a handle on my weight problem. I wanted to lose weight while still being able to maintain my style of eating. "A good trick if it can be done."

No salads and carrot stick for me! I'm a human, not a rabbit. I tried several ways to lose, but I always had one little problem — I never liked feeling hungry.

Why should I?

Even now I still get a little embarrassed when someone mentions the amount of food on my plate.

Listen. I like food.

And I like to eat.

And I like being thin.

Why not have it all?

For those of you who have read a LowFat Connection (LFC) brochure, you already recognize these introduction words.

It's exciting for me to have a part in this publication.

Yes, I lost 110 pounds in 14 months. That was SEVEN years ago and it is STILL OFF!

Like my brochure says, "My husband and I have never had it so good." Yes, he loved me before I lost the 110 lbs. My self-esteem and my self-confidence has greatly increased since my weight-loss experience. As a result, Frank and I have strengthened our marital relationship.

More Self-Esteem. . . Self-confidence!

NOTE FROM THE AUTHOR

As you will see, this book is written for the ordinary person wanting to lose weight in the plain, ordinary way of home-style cooking.

Also, I hope, out of my many years of checking out low-cal and low-fat cookbooks, that you will see some of the frustration I experienced.

It is time that the average person should be able to read a recipe and understand what the ingredients are in a recipe book.

I often wondered how we were supposed to buy and pre-pare ingredients when we have never heard of them!

The recipes in this book have been kept as simple as possible so that you can go to your own local grocer and shop as a normal person, and your budget will not be blown out of proportion.

During those last 14 months, seven years ago, I lost my 110 pounds through struggling with the holidays.

By including holiday menus with these recipes, I'm sure this will make your low-fat journey much easier.

NOTE: I would like to make a comment concerning name-brand products. Some brands I prefer to use because they both taste and work better. So, keep that in mind when you purchase your fat-free staple items. I have indicated my preferences on various recipes.

I would like to share an old Chinese proverb with you:

"Feed a man a fish and you feed him for a day. Teach a man HOW TO fish and you feed him for a lifetime."

By learning how to limit your fat grams, you, will be able to control your weight and health for life!

July 2, 1994
Natoma Riley

TABLE OF CONTENTS

The Holiday Express

The Fat-BUSting Bus

INTRODUCTION

Low-fat principles really work in your losing weight. In fact, it's very hard NOT to reach that conclusion from the various media resources whether it comes from television, articles or books.

Materials abound on the subject and value. You probably know the basics. There are three organic nutrients you hear about in losing weight: carbohydrates, proteins and fats. Your carbs provide energy to the body and comes from cereals, bread, pastries, tapioca and fruits. Proteins are used for growth, maintenance and repair of cells along with the manufacture of enzymes. They come from lean meats, eggs, milk, wheat, beans, peas and cheese.

Your fats provide energy too. They come from sources such as butter, cream, shortening, oils, cheese, margarine, nuts and meats.

Fats and oils yield more than twice as much energy as the carbs per unit weight. They can be absorbed into the bloodstream directly.

So, what's different about "counting fats"?

In the past, we were told first that if we watched our food groups, all would be okay; but people continued to gain weight. Then we were told that "starches" were the culprits, so we stayed away from them; but people still gained weight.

Then we were told "calories" are the villains. Watch your calories. Count them. But, still, Americans gained weight.

Think of all the diets Americans have tried over the years: Low calorie. Grapefruit diet. Rice diet. Low carbohydrate diet. Air Force diet. Stillman diet. Ayds Candy diet. Beverly Hills Doctors diet. Dallas Doctor's diet.

And think of the organizations involved: Weight Watchers. Jenny Craig. Nutri-System. Diet Center. Overeaters Anonymous. Herbalife. And many others.

Why do we need another one? Why the LowFat Connection?

Because our time has come, that's why. We're on the cutting edge. We're representing part of the latest findings in scientific research.

-how this book can help you-

I know your pain, your hurts, your frustrations.

I went through all of that some seven years ago.

This book can be of help for you.

In Section One, you will read about how I got started in this business.

It is about a weight-loss program that really works!

It shows you how low-fat counting really works for you and what's different about it from traditional programs. I tell you how I discovered this principle/concept in my own life.

Section Two is about eating. You'll find our recipes of low-fat homestyle cooking. They are easy to read and informative.

You'll see recipes for all seasons: Easter, Summer, Thanksgiving, Christmas and all of the ones in between.

Also, I've made it easier for you by dividing these recipes into groupings: meats, casseroles, veggies, salads, desserts and so forth.

In Section Three, you'll have the opportunity to learn how to plan your own seven day menu, much like we do in our business.

What we do at the LowFat Connection can be taught and learned. I bring to you some of the tricks of my trade that I've learned the hard way over the years.

Furthermore, there are things you need to know about menu planning.

You'll find a word, too, about fast foods.

And there will be a word about vacations.

Another way we have made it easy for you the reader is by indexing. We've indexed the recipes by alphabet, by titles, by groupings and by seasons.

That's hard to beat.

You'll enjoy it.

SECTION ONE

HOW AN OUTSIDER DESCRIBED MY WEIGHT-LOSS PROGRAM
"FAT-buster develops weight-loss plan"

The breaking point for Natoma Riley was when she broke the zipper while trying to get into her Size 22 jeans. Riley, who weighed 253 pounds, tried every diet remedy she could find. She lost patience, not weight.

"I was going to bed at night close to tears I was so hungry," recalled the 48-year-old Evansville grandmother. "I wanted my macaroni. I wanted fried chicken, beans and corn bread, the things I was raised on." She claims she got what she wanted, and she ended up 110 pounds lighter by changing the way she cooked things. "It's not the foods; it's what we're doing to them," said Riley, who lost the weight in 14 months. "The answer isn't to eat less but to eat different."

Six months ago, after keeping the weight off for six years and inspired by the response from the pan of low-fat lasagna she took to the gals at the beauty shop, she started marketing her weight-loss service.

She doesn't sell any food or liquid products. What she sells is a menu plan and support group membership.

Her business, The LowFat Connection, Inc., is based on counting fat grams; and she maintains 20 a day is the way to lose.

Fat. It's a big and bad word these days.

Fat is the buzzword on talk shows and on product labels at the supermarket. There are fat books on fat. There are fat profits being made on fat.

Riley is upfront that she is not a dietician or medical professional. She worked in hotels and for years was a desk clerk. "I lost weight and became a general manager. Was it all physical? No. It had to so with self-esteem," Riley said. Her style is homespun and her recipes homestyle.

"Good common sense. That's what it is. We all like the same things: macaroni and cheese, corn bread, cheesecake," she said.

She is fond of saying: "At the risk of sounding like Joan Rivers, 'Let's get real.'"

Riley maintains people aren't going to live on beets very long, and they aren't going to give up their comfort foods for very much longer.

"They think I've descended from heaven when I tell them they can have their coleslaw," said the self-proclaimed "fat-buster".

Her mission is to "defat" foods folks around here eat so they can retain normalcy at the supper table and serve one meal the whole family can eat.

Riley cites corn bread as an example of a simple recipe modification: "Put the yolk down the sink and put in two egg whites; use a tablespoon of applesauce instead of shortening; use skim milk." She also credits the many low-fat and no-fat products now available, but cautions dieters not to eat them with abandon. "You can gain weight on fat-free desserts," she notes.

Riley offers a basic 28-day meal plan . . . [along with a personalized plan]. Monthly membership for a new[s]letter and bi-weekly support group meetings, led by her in Evansville, Newburgh and Mount Vernon. . . .Her husband, Frank, pastor of Church of Christ in Mount Vernon, lends a hand behind the scenes and at meetings.

Riley says her weight-loss program isn't for everybody.

"Some work out and some don't," she said. It also takes dedication. "You have to want to do it."

For personalized plans, Riley will contact restaurants to get the fat gram count of dieters' favorite dishes, then devise ways to defat items, such as by the use of lower-fat condiments. When a weight-loss goal is obtained, more fat grams are added back into the dieter's fat budget.

Riley said there are 117 people in her program [206 as of late August, 1994 F.R.] mainly women, ranging in age from 15 to 75. Their menu musts range from pickled pigs' feet to candy bars. She tells of the teenager who "has to have a Snickers. I give her one every three days."

Meal items on the plan are listed by portion size and fat grams, and dieters have free reign to "borrow from Peter to pay Paul," she said.

Sue Essary of Mount Vernon said she has bartered away 32 pounds since joining LowFat Connection in March. "If I know I'm going to have a nice steak for supper, I will take a nice steak for supper. I will take my fat grams for that day and plunk it all on that steak," said Essary, adding she has about 130 pounds more to go. "The fantastic part is that I can eat whatever I want," Essary said. "I just fix it different. I just whack off fat grams to make up for anything I eat."

Caution should be used when whacking off fat grams for too long, advises Monica Hochgesang, chief clinical dietitian at St. Mary's Medical Center [Evansville, Indiana, F.R.]. She said there's a slight chance of having a vitamin deficiency of A,D,E and K, the fat-soluble vitamins that are absorbed in the bloodstream, if a dieter has only 20 grams of fat per day for longer than three months.

Hochgesang said the American Dietetic Association recommends having 30 percent of total calories come from fat sources. For someone on an 1,800-calorie diet, that would mean 60 grams of fat a day.

Hochgesang, who serves as an external consultant for Riley with some diet plans, noted Riley's program does call for an eventual increase in fat grams. "There is a population out there that she can be a real valuable asset to," she said. "She gives them one-on-one consultation and provides them with a support group, and those two keys are very important in weight loss."

Dr. James Heinrich, who has attempted about every diet program in town, refers to Riley as his "personal trainer for diet". The orthopedic surgeon said he recommends a low-fat diet to patients who need to lose weight. "If they say, 'I don't know what that is,' I tell them, 'I know a lady who does,'" he said.

Heinrich said Riley's program is "inexpensive, and you lose if you really do go on it." If you stray, you wind up like him, facing the scale and Riley two pounds heavier at a bi-weekly weigh-in.

His wife, Anne, finds the Riley plan practical because it means fixing one meal that everybody in the family can and will eat. "It's not far off from what we ate before," she said. "It's just a different way of cooking."

Source: Andrea Brown,
"FAT-buster develops weight-loss plan",
The Evansville Press, June 15, 1994, p.16.

TESTIMONIES

Now you'll read of some "testimonies" by some already
in the LFC PLAN. They are just like most of you — plain,
ordinary people with plain, ordinary food tastes.
Consider what they have to say about our plan and see
if you can identify with any of their struggles and
victories.

May 19, 1994

"Dear Mrs. Natoma Riley:

I became a "Fatbuster" in March, 1994. I would like to take
this opportunity to share my success story with you. I have
lost over 25 pounds without counting calories!

In the past, with other programs I was always hungry, and I
was constantly in the yo-yo syndrome with my weight.
Now, I'm able to eat out with my family at least 3 times a
week, prepare my family's favorite dinners, and I'm still
losing weight! I can't believe it.

When the Lowfat Connection came into my life, there was
finally someone who knew the importance of listing plain
homestyle foods in my menu plan.

Thanks again, Mrs. Riley and the Lowfat Connection.

Mrs. Gale R."
Mt. Vernon, Indiana

May 24, 1994
"Mrs. Natoma Riley

Thank you so much for starting your program, "The Lo-Fat
[sic] Connection" and the support group in Mt. Vernon. To
me, it is an answer to an ongoing battle. The 30 lbs. I have
lost since March, prove the plan works. I have tried to lose
weight on other plans with group support, and was not able
to stick with them for any length of time because of
frustration of measuring, weighing, and doing without my
favorite foods. Now, I'm learning a new way to cook my old
favorite recipes and getting new ones each week at
the meeting that are delicious.

Our support group's sharing of personal solutions to our
common dietary problems plus your personal touch of being
there anytime I need a friendly boost or word of
encouragement, are answers to prayer. It is great to know
that I'm not alone in the 'Battle of the Bulge' but that
someone who has won a similar battle is leading the parade.

Thanks again for all your help.

Sincerely yours,
Sue E."
Mt. Vernon, Indiana

*"At LFC we
take the fat out
and keep the
flavor in!"*

"What I like so much about this program is the fact that you get to eat so much. I never go hungry. I have always loved to eat out at fast food restaurants. I was thrilled when I found that I could eat fast food and still follow this program. I don't get to eat as much of the fast food as I used to but it makes me feel great to know that this is not a complete 'no no'. I'm eating at home a lot more than I use [sic] and my eating habits have improved greatly. I used to be a junk food junky. I feel wonderful knowing that I am putting food into my body that is supplying it with nutrients and vitamins rather than fats and cholesterol. I am still enjoying my favorite foods like fried potatoes, salmon patties and fried chicken. I prepare them a little differently but the flavor is just as good. I now read every label of every product that I purchase.

The first time I weighed in I had lost a total of nine pounds over a period of two and a half weeks. I just couldn't believe I had lost that much weight in that amount of time. It has been about two months since I started and I have lost a total of 15 pounds.

This program has had a positive effect on my life. I'm eating out, eating snacks and losing weight. You can't ask for more than that.

Brenda H."
Evansville, Indiana

SECTION TWO

The Holiday Express

and
The Fat BUSting Bus

SECTION TWO

The Recipes Of Low-Fat HomeStyle Cooking

Before you read the specific recipes listed in the following pages, it can be helpful to you as the reader to access the following information.

NOTE: You may use salt and pepper to your taste and/or requirements.

SLOW CROCK POT COOKING

To convert favorite recipes for slow cookers

REGULAR TIMING	*SLOW COOKER*
15 to 30 minutes..............	1 1/2 to 2 1/2 hours on high or 4 to 8 hours on low
35 to 45 minutes..............	3 to 4 hours on high or 6 to 10 hours on low
50 minutes to 3 hours......	4 to 6 hours on high or 8 to 16 hours on low

TO TEST COOKER TEMPERATURE- TIMING Fill cooker half-full of cold tap water. Heat, covered on high for 2 1/2 hours. If water boils in less time, reduce recipe cooking time. If it takes more than three hours to boil, add cooking time.

FOR SAFETY- Use pot in a safe place where cord is up out of the way. Never store food in crockery pot. Sudden temperature changes can crack ceramic liners. 180 degrees F is a minimum safe cooking temperature. Read and use cooker instructions carefully.

TO SERVE CROCKERY COOKING- Garnish with parsley, carrot curls, crushed corn chips, tomatoes, sauces, olives, pimentos, mint leaves, lemon or orange slices.

ADDITIONAL CROCKERY COOKING HINTS- Use a timer for starting pot and cooking when you aren't around. Crossed strips of folded aluminum foil under roast will let you lift it quickly and safely to serving dish. Most recipes for low temperatures can be prepared in half the time on high. A slow pot is excellent for dips, hot punch, sauces, and as a bun warmer.

COOKING TERMS

Blend -   Stir ingredients lightly until well mixed.

Broil -   Follow directions for broiling on kitchen range, charcoal or gas grill.

Cream -   Beat shortening with a spoon or fork until spreadable consistency.

Marinate -   To allow a food to stand in a liquid such as oil and vinegar, French dressing or seasoned vinegar. Time improves flavor and tenderizes meats.

Sauté -   To cook slowly in a small amount of margarine.
(I heat my fat-free margarine in a microwave before using it in my pan. Fat-free margarine does not do well if you try to melt it first in a pan.)

FATS PER SERVING: Sometimes, you'll find two numbers mentioned at the end of each recipe concerning FATS PER SERVING. The first number is for the first meat mentioned in the ingredients. For example, on page 46 the numbers are "6-3" FATS PER SERVING. The text lists "ground round" or "turkey." Six is for the "ground round" and three is for "turkey." Other examples are found on page 55, 128 and131.

NOTE: The ingredient in recipes that call for "Bread Crumbs" is FAT-FREE bread crumbled into small pieces. FAT-FREE Parmesan cheese is made by a famous weight-loss brand.

TABLE OF SUBSTITUTIONS

Now a days, there are plenty of substitutes for the older "fat" ingredients.

One can use fat-free margarines for butter, or lite or fat-free whipped toppings such as Dream Whip for the older whipped toppings.

There are now fat-free creme cheeses for items such as Philadelphia Cream Cheese.

Skim milk can substitute for regular milk.

For oil in your baking, you can substitute applesauce.

For seasoning items such as pinto beans, you can use a famous brand name such as Lipton Onion Soup Mix.

Eggs now have a substitute with products such as Egg Beaters.

More and more, the food industry is responding to consumer demands for more "fat-free" products. As you read the following recipes, keep all of this in mind.

RECIPES
FOR ALL SEASONS

How do I get started?

At LFC, our program is designed around 20 fat grams per day for our people. Why 20?

1. All recommendations I've seen on the subject states that the standard daily fat gram intake for women is 20-40 and 30-60 for men.

2. We feel that choosing 20 gives you room for error, thus making it easier for you to lose weight even if you count wrong.

Remember, this is only the beginning when you are losing weight. It is not the "maintenance" side of the program. Once you've achieved your desired weight, you need to begin a maintenance program.

Now that I've lost it, how do I keep it off?

An easy way of figuring out just how much "fat grams" you should have in a weight control plan, use the following formulas:

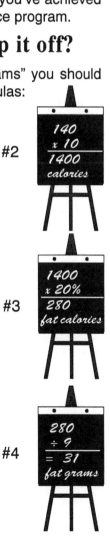

I. Decide on your goal or desired weight.

2. Take that figure and multiply it by ten to get a "calorie" intake amount.   #2

3. Then multiply that by twenty percent (20%) to get a "fat gram" calorie number.

4. Divide by nine to convert the fat calories into fat grams.

An example: #3

• You weigh 190 pounds. Your desired goal or weight is 140 pounds.

• 140 X 10 is 1,400 which is the calorie intake amount.

• 1,400 multiplied by twenty percent (20%) is 280 fat calories.

• 280 divided by nine is 31 fat grams.   #4

In maintenance, one can often have a range of 30 to 60 fat grams per day, depending, of course, upon several factors.

Again, we're not doctors nor dietitians.

HIGH-FAT FOOD ALTERNATIVES

In this day and time, there are plenty of alternatives one may use for the older "fat" ingredients that so many of us were raised up on.

OLD WAY	ALTERNATIVE
butter margarines	FAT FREE margarine, jam apple-butter, preserves
cakes, pie cookies, and pasteries	FAT FREE cookies, angel food cake, baked apple, and other similar items
fried foods	Roast, steam broil, mirowave or bake meats and vegetables
oils, salad sour cream mayonnaise	FAT FREE salad dressings Low-Fat or Non-fat plain yogurt, mustard and reduced-calorie salad dressings
snack crackers or chips	Low-fat, air popped or microwaved popcorn, FAT FREE pretzels, rice cakes, and crisp breads
whole milk	1% skim milk, non-fat dry milk

Consider this material through the following metaphor.

You are getting on a "fat-busting" bus, and you are going to ride with us as we travel down the road and see different groupings available to us.

The first thing you'll see is "appetizers", then "caseroles" and "desserts". Don't forget the "meats". You've wondered about them for a long time. Oh, I almost forgot. Towards the back of the bus you can see "pasta/grains" and "salads" and "veggies". Who has not heard of these items?

I'll be your tour guide as you travel. It will be an easy ride for you, and enjoyment can be yours.

So, enjoy the ride on the "fat-busting" bus!

APPETIZERS

CHEESE DIP FOR BAKED POTATOES

1 8-ounce FAT FREE cream cheese
4 tablespoons skim milk
1 tablespoon minced onion
1 teaspoon salt
1/4 teaspoon garlic powder

METHOD:
Mix above ingredients together and, if too thick, add a bit
more skim milk.
Serve over baked potatoes instead of sour cream.

MAKES 1 cup

FATS PER SERVING: FAT FREE

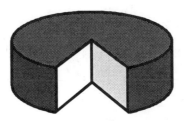

Notes: _____

Rating For This Recipe
❑ Poor ❑ Fair
❑ Good ❑ Excellent

_____

_____

_____

CURRY DIP

1 cup FAT FREE Miracle Whip
Dash of tobasco sauce
1/4 teaspoon garlic salt
3 tablespoons catsup
1 tablespoon Worcestershire sauce
2 teaspoons curry powder
2 teaspoons onion salt

METHOD:
Mix well.
Allow to sit several hours to blend flavors.
Serve with fresh vegetable slices or sticks.

MAKES one cup

FATS PER SERVING: FAT FREE

Notes: _____

_____

_____

_____

Rating For This Recipe	
❑ Poor	❑ Fair
❑ Good	❑ Excellent

DELICIOUS DAIRY DIP

1 8-ounce FAT FREE cream cheese, softened
1/2 cup FAT FREE sour cream
4 packs sugar substitute
1 teaspoon LITE brown sugar
1 tablespoon lite maple-flavored pancake syrup

METHOD:
Mix all ingredients in a small bowl.
Chill.
Serve with fresh fruit, a real lo-cal treat.

MAKES one cup

FATS PER SERVING: FAT FREE

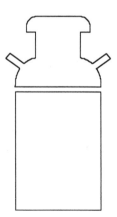

<table>
<tr><td>Rating For This Recipe</td></tr>
<tr><td>❑ Poor ❑ Fair</td></tr>
<tr><td>❑ Good ❑ Excellent</td></tr>
</table>

Notes: _____
_____
_____
_____

FAT FREE VEGGIES DIPS

I. 1 8-ounce FAT FREE cream cheese
    1/4 cup FAT FREE Catalina salad dressing
    Dash of tobasco sauce
    Dash of reconstituted lemon juice

    METHOD:
    Beat above ingredients until fluffy.
    Use with fresh veggies, sticks or slices, pretzels,
    NO FAT Tortilla chips.
    MAKES 1 CUP FAT FREE Dip

II. 1 package famous brand dry onion soup mix
    1 8-ounce container FAT FREE plain yogurt

    METHOD:
    Mix above ingredients well.
    Refrigerate for several hours.
    Use as dip with fresh vegetable sticks, pretzels or
    NO FAT tortilla chips.
    MAKES 1 CUP FAT FREE Dip

III. 1 packet famous brand dry vegetable soup mix
    1 8-ounce container FAT FREE sour cream

    METHOD:
    Mix sour cream and soup mix thoroughly.
    Use as dip with fresh vegetables, pretzels,
    NO FAT tortilla chips.
    MAKES 1 CUP FAT FREE Dip

Notes: _____

_____

_____

_____

Rating For This Recipe	
❏ Poor	❏ Fair
❏ Good	❏ Excellent

FAT FREE POTATO CHIP DIP

Small package FAT FREE cream cheese
1/3 cup catsup
2 tablespoons FAT FREE French dressing
1/2 teaspoon grated onion
1/4 teaspoon salt

METHOD:
Mix above ingredients well.
Allow to sit several hours to blend flavors.
Chill.

MAKES one cup

FATS PER SERVING: FAT FREE

"I Like Food!"

Rating For This Recipe	Notes: _____
☐ Poor ☐ Fair	_____
☐ Good ☐ Excellent	_____

FRUIT PUNCH #1

1 large can pineapple juice
1 cup sugar
1 large can frozen orange juice
Add water to make 1 gallon.
Cool treat for summer!

METHOD:
Mix all ingredients. Stir well.
Refrigerate.

SERVES: 8

FATS PER SERVING: FAT FREE

FRUIT PUNCH #2

1/2 gallon FAT FREE pineapple sherbet
Lemon soda - 1 quart
3 quarts ginger ale

METHOD:
Mix all ingredients. Stir well.
Refrigerate.

SERVES: 8

FATS PER SERVING: FAT FREE

Notes: _____

_____

_____

_____

FRUIT DIP

1 8-ounce container FAT FREE plain yogurt
Grated rind of medium size lime
Sweetener to taste

METHOD:
Mix above ingredients and
refrigerate several hours to blend flavors.
Skewer fresh fruit (such as apple slices, pineapple chunks,
oranges, etc.) on wooden skewers or hors d'oeuvre picks.
Arrange on attractive tray and serve with dip.

MAKES I CUP FAT FREE Dip

Rating For This Recipe	Notes: _____
❏ Poor ❏ Fair	_____
❏ Good ❏ Excellent	_____

FRUIT DRESSING

3 tablespoons cornstarch
6 tablespoons sugar
1/8 teaspoon salt
1/4 cup lemon juice
1/3 cup pineapple juice
1 tablespoon orange juice frozen concentrate
1 packet dry whipped topping made with skim milk
as directed on the package

METHOD:
In a saucepan mix the cornstarch, sugar and salt.
Slowly add the fruit juices stirring until well mixed.
Place over medium heat and bring to a boil.
Add orange juice concentrate and reduce heat.
Continue stirring until thickened. Cool.
Fold into the dry whipped topping. Chill.
Excellent with FRUIT ON A STICK.

FATS PER SERVING: FAT FREE

FRUIT ON A STICK

Thread whole strawberries, honeydew melon,
cantaloupe melon, kiwi fruit, any fresh fruit
of your choice on wooden skewers.
Dip in the above dressing.

FATS PER SERVING: FAT FREE

Notes: _____

_____

_____

_____

Rating For This Recipe	
❏ Poor	❏ Fair
❏ Good	❏ Excellent

GUILTLESS CHEESE POTATO CRISPS

Preheat oven to 375 degrees.
4-6 medium potatoes scrubbed and cut in wedges about 1/4 thick.
Salt to taste.
1 1/2 cups finely shredded FAT FREE sharp Cheddar cheese
2 cups crushed crisp-rice cereal
Paprika
2 egg whites, slightly beaten

METHOD:
Spray jelly roll pan with butter
Flavored non-stick cooking spray
Dip potato wedges in beaten egg whites and arrange in a single layer on prepared pan.
Sprinkle with salt, then with cheese.
Sprinkle crushed cereal evenly over all.
Garnish with paprika.
Bake 20-25 minutes.

SERVES: 4-6

FATS PER SERVING: FAT FREE

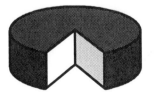

Notes: _____

_____

Rating For This Recipe
❑ Poor ❑ Fair

❑ Good ❑ Excellent

HEARTY SPINACH DIP

2 10-ounce packages of FROZEN spinach,
thawed and squeezed dry.
1 package famous brand dry vegetable soup mix
16-ounce FAT FREE sour cream

METHOD:
Mix well and allow to sit overnight.
Stir well before serving with FAT FREE pretzels, fresh
vegetables or FAT FREE tortilla chips.

MAKES one cup

FATS PER SERVING: FAT FREE

Notes: _____

_____

_____

_____

Rating For This Recipe	
❑ Poor	❑ Fair
❑ Good	❑ Excellent

ONION DIP

1 cup FAT FREE plain yogurt or FAT FREE sour cream
2 tablespoons famous brand dry onion soup mix

METHOD:
Mix together and allow to sit
2-3 hours to blend flavors.
Serve with fresh vegetables, pretzels or FAT FREE
tortilla chips.

MAKES one cup

FATS PER SERVING: FAT FREE

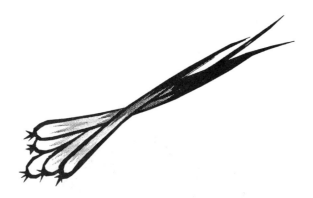

Rating For This Recipe	Notes: _____
❏ Poor ❏ Fair	_____
❏ Good ❏ Excellent	_____

SAVORY STEAK RUB

1 tablespoon famous brand FAT FREE margarine
1 tablespoon sweet basil
2 teaspoons garlic powder
2 teaspoons thyme
1 teaspoon crushed dried rosemary
3/4 teaspoon dried oregano

METHOD:
Combine all the spices and mix well.
Rub over steaks before grilling or broiling for a delicious,
different taste.

Yields 1/4 cup.
Store in airtight container.

FATS PER SERVING: FAT FREE

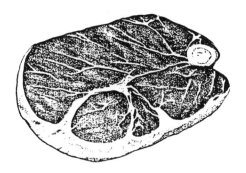

Notes: _____

_____

_____

_____

Rating For This Recipe	
❏ Poor	❏ Fair
❏ Good	❏ Excellent

PARTY CLAM DIP

1 8-ounce package FAT FREE cream cheese
1/2 cup FAT FREE Miracle Whip
1/4 cup skim milk
Tobasco sauce to taste
1 envelope famous brand vegetable soup mix
2 6-1/2-ounce cans minced clams, drained
1/2 teaspoon lemon juice

METHOD:
Mix well and allow to stand at least 4 hours to
blend flavors.

MAKES one cup

FATS PER SERVING: FAT FREE

Rating For This Recipe
❏ Poor ❏ Fair
❏ Good ❏ Excellent

Notes: _____

_____

_____

_____

TOSTITO DIP

1 can FAT FREE refried beans
1 6-ounce (2/3 cups) FAT FREE sour cream
8 ounces FAT FREE Cheddar cheese
1 package taco seasoning mix

METHOD:
Mix all of the above ingredients and either
bake at 350 degrees for about 20 minutes,
OR microwave on high until it's hot.
Serve with FAT FREE tortilla chips.

MAKES two cups

FATS PER SERVING: TRACE

"I'm not a doctor nor a dietitian."

Notes: _____

_____

_____

_____

Rating For This Recipe
❏ Poor ❏ Fair
❏ Good ❏ Excellent

VEGETABLE DIP

1 8-ounce container of FAT FREE sour cream
1 package famous brand dry vegetable soup mix

METHOD:
In small bowl, mix dry soup
mixture and FAT FREE sour cream and allow
flavors to blend.
Serve with fresh vegetables, FAT FREE pretzels or
FAT FREE tortilla chips.

MAKES one cup

FATS PER SERVING: FAT FREE

Rating For This Recipe	Notes: _____
❑ Poor ❑ Fair	_____
❑ Good ❑ Excellent	_____

Notes: _____

_____

_____

_____

Rating For This Recipe
❏ Poor   ❏ Fair
❏ Good   ❏ Excellent

CASSEROLES:

ASPARAGUS CASSEROLE

2 medium size cans asparagus
2 cups white sauce
1/2 cup almonds (slivered)
1 1/2 cups grated cheese
10 crushed FAT FREE crackers
White sauce:
4 tablespoons famous brand FAT FREE margarine
4 tablespoons flour
1 teaspoon salt
1/2 teaspoon pepper
2 cups skim milk

METHOD:
Melt margarine, add flour, salt and pepper.
Stir until blended. Gradually add milk and stir until thick and creamy.
Place layer of drained asparagus in casserole.
Cover with 1/2 of cheese, almonds and sauce.
Add remainder of asparagus, cheese, etc. and sprinkle top with FAT FREE cracker crumbs.
Bake 20 or 30 minutes at 350 degrees.

SERVES: 8

FATS PER SERVING: 7

Rating For This Recipe
❑ Poor ❑ Fair
❑ Good ❑ Excellent

Notes: _____

_____

_____

_____

BROCCOLI CASSEROLE

1 1/2 cups frozen broccoli, thawed
6 ounces of egg substitute
3 tablespoons flour
1 cup famous brand FAT FREE margarine
2 cups FAT FREE cottage cheese (small curd)
1 cup FAT FREE Cheddar cheese, cut up
1 green onion (tops and all) chopped
Lite cooking spray

METHOD:
Mix all ingredients with mixer until well blended.
Pour in sprayed casserole dish and bake at 350 degrees for
1 hour or until golden brown and bubbly.

SERVES:4

FATS PER SERVING: TRACE

Notes: _____

_____

_____

_____

Rating For This Recipe	
☐ Poor	☐ Fair
☐ Good	☐ Excellent

BUSY DAY CASSEROLE

4 or 5 medium potatoes, peeled and sliced
1 large onion, sliced
1 pound ground round OR turkey breast
1 green pepper
1 cup grated FAT FREE sharp Cheddar cheese
1 can tomato soup

METHOD:
Brown and drain ground meat.
In a sprayed 2-quart casserole dish, spread one
layer of potatoes, one layer of onion and
one layer of ground meat, one layer green pepper,
one layer of cheese.
Pour soup over all.
Cover and bake 45 minutes in a 350-degree oven.
Uncover bake 15 minutes longer.

SERVES: 4

FATS PER SERVING: 6-4

Rating For This Recipe
☐ Poor ☐ Fair
☐ Good ☐ Excellent

Notes: _____
_____
_____
_____

CAN-CAN CASSEROLE

Combine in 1 1/2 quart casserole:
1 can (10 1/2-ounce) condensed cream of chicken soup
1 1/2 cups water
1 can (12-ounce) boned chicken (white)
1 can (10 1/2-ounce) condensed cream of celery soup
1 1/3 cups packaged precooked rice

Cover and bake in 400-degree oven for 25 minutes.
Uncover and stir well.
Top with sliced onion rings.
Leave uncovered and return to oven for 5 minutes.

SERVES: 6

FATS PER SERVING: 7

CREAM
OF
CHICKEN

CREAM
OF
CELERY

Notes: _____

_____

_____

_____

Rating For This Recipe
❏ Poor   ❏ Fair
❏ Good   ❏ Excellent

CHICKEN CASSEROLE

Preheat oven to 375 degrees
2 cups cooked chicken, finely chopped
1 cup FAT FREE soft bread crumbs
2 tablespoons parsley
2 tablespoons finely chopped celery
2 teaspoons salt
1/2 cup egg substitute (equals 2 eggs)
1 cup skim milk

METHOD:
Spray loaf pan with non-stick cooking spray.
In a large bowl, mix all of the ingredients thoroughly.
Pat into the loaf pan and bake for 30 minutes.
Let stand 5 minutes, tip onto serving platter and slice.

SERVES: 6-8

FATS PER SERVING: 5

Rating For This Recipe
❑ Poor ❑ Fair
❑ Good ❑ Excellent

Notes: _____

_____

_____

_____

CHILI PIE WITH RICE CRUST

1/4 cup egg substitute (equals 1 egg)
2 cups cooked rice
2 ounces shredded FAT FREE Cheddar cheese

METHOD:

Spray a 9-inch pie pan with non-stick spray
Mix ingredients thoroughly and press in bottom and
up the sides of pie pan.
Bake at 425 degrees for 20-25 minutes or until lightly browned.
Remove from oven.
REDUCE HEAT OF OVEN TO 350 DEGREES

1/2 pound cooked and drained ground round
1/2 cup chopped onion
1/2 cup chopped green pepper
1 clove garlic, minced
1 can kidney beans (or Chili beans), drained
1 #2 can tomatoes, drained and chopped
I teaspoon chili powder (or more to taste)
1-2 drops tobasco sauce

METHOD:

Saute onion, pepper and garlic in sprayed skillet.
Add rest of ingredients and cook until liquid is reduced by half.
Pour into the rice shell and bake 20-25 minutes then remove
from oven and sprinkle top with 2-ounces more of the
FAT FREE Cheddar cheese.
Return to oven until cheese melts, 5-10 minutes.
Allow to stand 5 minutes before cutting. *Delicious!*

SERVES: 4

FATS PER SERVING: 8

Notes: _____

_____

_____

_____

Rating For This Recipe	
❏ Poor	❏ Fair
❏ Good	❏ Excellent

CORN CASSEROLE

Preheat oven to 350 degrees
1 box famous brand corn muffin mlx
8 ounces of egg substitute
1 can cream-style corn
1 can whole kernel corn undrained
8 ounces FAT FREE sour cream
3 tablespoons famous brand FAT FREE margarine

METHOD:
Melt 3 tablespoons FAT FREE margarine in 2-quart glass
dish in microwave or in oven as it preheats.
In a large bowl, mix other ingredients,
stirring well until well mixed.
Pour into 2-quart dish containing margarine.
Diced onions may be placed on top
if desired. (optional)
Bake, uncovered, for 1 hour

SERVES: 4-6

FATS PER SERVING: TRACE

Rating For This Recipe
❏ Poor ❏ Fair
❏ Good ❏ Excellent

Notes: _____

_____

_____

_____

FRIDAY'S DAY CASSEROLE

1 pound ground turkey breast
1 6-ounce package macaroni
3 tablespoons famous brand FAT FREE margarine
3 tablespoons flour
1/3 cup chopped pepper (green or red)
1 1/2 cups skim milk
1 cup grated FAT FREE Cheddar cheese

METHOD:
Cook macaroni in salted water 7 minutes.
Drain.
Fry meat and green pepper in margarine;
add flour and blend.
Add milk.
Cook until thick, stirring constantly.
Add 3/4 cup of cheese.
Stir in macaroni and pour into sprayed casserole dish.
Top with remaining cheese.
Bake in moderate oven 350 degrees for 30 minutes.

SERVES: 4

FATS PER SERVING: 4

Notes: _____

_____

_____

_____

Rating For This Recipe	
❏ Poor	❏ Fair
❏ Good	❏ Excellent

GREEN BEAN CASSEROLE

Mix together all these ingredients:

2 cans green beans (French style)
1 tablespoon famous brand FAT FREE margarine
Dash salt and pepper
1/4 cup diced onions
8 ounces mushroom soup
Dash Worcestershire sauce
1 tablespoon flour
1 cup grated FAT FREE Cheddar cheese

METHOD:

After mixing all the above ingredients, sprinkle 1 cup of
grated FAT FREE Cheddar cheese on top.
Bake 45 to 50 minutes at 375 degrees.
The last 5 minutes of cooking, sprinkle top with
onion rings and put back in oven.

SERVES: 4

FATS PER SERVING: 1

Rating For This Recipe
❏ Poor ❏ Fair
❏ Good ❏ Excellent

Notes: _____

_____

_____

_____

LASAGNA CASSEROLE

Preheat oven to 375 degrees.
1 pound LEAN ground round OR turkey
1 pound can tomatoes
3 8-ounce cans tomato sauce
1/2 cup onion
1/4 cup green pepper
1 1/2 teaspoons salt
1/4 teaspoon pepper
1/3 teaspoon oregano
Lasagna noodles, cooked and drained
1 12-ounce package FAT FREE Mozzarella cheese

METHOD:
Brown and drain ground meat.
Add tomatoes, tomato sauce, onion, green peppers,
and oregano.
Simmer about 1 hour.
Spoon 1/4 of the sauce into a 13 x 9 x 2 baking dish that
has been sprayed with a non-stick cooking spray.
Arrange a layer of noodles over sauce and sprinkle half
the cheese over them.
Repeat layers.
Bake for 30-45 minutes.
Allow to stand 5 minutes before serving.

SERVES: 8

FATS PER SERVING: 6-3

Notes: _____

_____

_____

_____

Rating For This Recipe	
❏ Poor	❏ Fair
❏ Good	❏ Excellent

NIGHT BEFORE CASSEROLE

1/2 pound thin sliced package of 94% FAT FREE ham
12 slices FAT FREE bread
6 slices FAT FREE American cheese
Prepared mustard
1 carton egg substitute (equals 4 eggs)
3 cups skim milk
1/2 can cream of mushroom soup, undiluted
Dash Worcestershire sauce
Dash tobasco sauce
1/3 cup skim milk

METHOD:
Spread mustard on 6 slices of the bread, after removing crusts.
Place in the bottom of a 9 x 13 baking dish that has been
sprayed with butter-flavored cooking spray. Top each piece of
bread with a slice of the FAT FREE cheese, then a layer of the
thin sliced ham.
Spread mustard on other 6 slices of bread, after removing
crusts, and place on the ham slices.
Mix with an electric mixer the 3 cups of milk and the carton
of egg substitute.
Pour over all and cover with foil. Refrigerate overnight.
Bake the next day at 300 degrees for 1 hour.

Let stand 5 minutes before serving.

Meanwhile, mix 1/2 can of soup with the 1/3 cup milk and
tobasco and Worcestershire sauces and heat to boiling.
Serve over casserole. *Great for Sunday breakfast.*

SERVES: 6-8

FATS PER SERVING: Less than 2

Rating For This Recipe	Notes: _____
❏ Poor ❏ Fair	_____
❏ Good ❏ Excellent	_____
	_____

NOODLE CASSEROLE

1 package small EGGLESS noodles cooked
8-ounce carton FAT FREE sour cream
1 1/2 cups FAT FREE cottage cheese (small curd)
8 tablespoons famous brand FAT FREE margarine
Famous weight-loss brand FAT FREE Parmesan cheese

METHOD:
Cook and drain noodles (salted), fold in other ingredients.
Add margarine to hot noodles.
Place in casserole.
Sprinkle with FAT FREE Parmesan cheese on top.
Bake at 350 degrees until hot and bubbly.

SERVES: 4

FATS PER SERVING: 2

Notes: _____

_____

_____

_____

Rating For This Recipe	
❏ Poor	❏ Fair
❏ Good	❏ Excellent

NOODLES SUPREME

1/2 bag (1 pound) EGGLESS noodles
1 cup FAT FREE sour cream
1 pound FAT FREE cottage cheese
1 tablespoon chives
Famous weight-loss brand FAT FREE Parmesan cheese
paprika

METHOD:
Cook EGGLESS noodles in salted boiling water until tender.
Drain, rinse with cold water.
Add rest of ingredients and place in 2-quart casserole dish,
sprayed with butter-flavored cooking spray.
Bake 35-45 minutes or until bubbly and brown.
Preheat oven to 350 degrees.
Sprinkle casserole with Parmesan cheese and paprika.

SERVES: 6-8

FATS PER SERVING: TRACE

Rating For This Recipe	Notes: _____
❑ Poor ❑ Fair	_____
❑ Good ❑ Excellent	_____
	_____

RICE CASSEROLE

1 cup onion, chopped
4 cups cooked rice
2 cups FAT FREE sour cream
1 bay leaf, crumbled
1 cup FAT FREE cottage cheese
1 teaspoon salt
1/2 teaspoon pepper
1 4-ounce can green chilies, drained and chopped
2 cups FAT FREE shredded Cheddar cheese

METHOD:
Spray a skillet with non-stick cooking spray.
Saute onion over low heat until clear.
Spray a 2-quart casserole with butter-flavored cooking spray.
Mix all the ingredients EXCEPT the chilies and the cheese. Mix well.
Layer one half of the rice mixture, chilies, then cheese.
Repeat. Bake uncovered for 25 minutes at 350 degrees.

SERVES: 6

FATS PER SERVING: FAT FREE

Notes: _____

_____

_____

_____

Rating For This Recipe	
❑ Poor	❑ Fair
❑ Good	❑ Excellent

SOUP & NOODLE CASSEROLE

Small package EGGLESS noodles
1 can cream of mushroom soup
1 pound ground turkey breast
1 green pepper
1 can tomato soup
1 onion
2 cans evaporated skim milk

METHOD:
Cook EGGLESS noodles.
Add browned meat, onion and green pepper.
Add soups and milk.
Bake if desired or heat thoroughly.

SERVES: 6

FATS PER SERVING: 4

Rating For This Recipe
❑ Poor ❑ Fair
❑ Good ❑ Excellent

Notes: _____

_____

_____

_____

SQUASH CASSEROLE

2 pounds yellow crooked-neck squash
1 large onion
1 large green pepper, chopped
1 can famous brand mushroom soup
Salt and pepper to taste

METHOD:
Cut and wash unpeeled squash in 1/2 inch slices.
Add chopped onion and pepper to 1 cup water and
boil until done.
Drain. Add soup and salt and pepper.
Heat and serve.

SERVES: 4

FATS PER SERVING: 2

"I don't have to feel hungry all the time."

Notes: _____
_____
_____
_____

Rating For This Recipe	
❏ Poor	❏ Fair
❏ Good	❏ Excellent

SWEET POTATO CASSEROLE

3 cups mashed sweet potatoes
1/2 cup sugar
1/2 cup egg substitute
1 teaspoon vanilla
4 tablespoons famous brand FAT FREE margarine

METHOD:
Mix together, put into sprayed casserole dish.
Top with:
Brown sugar substitute — should equal 1 cup of brown sugar
1/3 cup flour
1/3 cup FAT FREE famous brand margarine

METHOD:
Rub above ingredients together and sprinkle over
sweet potatoes.
Bake at 350 degrees for 30 minutes.

SERVES: 6

FATS PER SERVING: FAT FREE
WATCH THOSE CALORIES!

Rating For This Recipe
❑ Poor ❑ Fair
❑ Good ❑ Excellent

Notes: _____
_____
_____
_____

VEGETABLE CASSEROLE

1 small package baby limas, cooked
1 can whole kernel corn, drained
2 tablespoons famous brand FAT FREE margarine
1 can cream of mushroom soup
1 small can pimentos
1 onion, chopped
1/2 cup shredded FAT FREE cheese
2 cups FAT FREE bread crumbs

METHOD:
Sauté onion in margarine.
Add limas, corn, pimentos and mix all together with shredded cheese.
Pour mushroom soup over this (undiluted).
Pour into casserole dish and sprinkle bread crumbs.
Spray top with butter-flavored cooking spray.
Bake at 350 degrees until bubbly.

SERVES: 6

FATS PER SERVING: 1

Notes: _____
_____
_____
_____

Rating For This Recipe	
❑ Poor	❑ Fair
❑ Good	❑ Excellent

VEGETABLE MEAT PIE

Preheat oven to 350 degrees.
1 pound ground round OR turkey
1 cup famous brand bran Chex cereal crushed
1/4 cup egg substitute OR 1 egg white
1/2 cup catsup
1 teaspoon salt
1 teaspoon onion powder
1/4 teaspoon pepper
1/2 teaspoon chili powder
1 10-ounce package frozen mixed vegetables,
cooked and drained

METHOD:
Mix all of the above ingredients together and
let sit for 5 minutes.
Press gently into sprayed 9-inch pie plate or casserole dish.
Bake uncovered about 30 minutes.
Let stand 5 or 10 minutes before serving.

SERVES: 8

FATS PER SERVING: 6-3

Rating For This Recipe
❑ Poor ❑ Fair
❑ Good ❑ Excellent

Notes: _____
_____
_____
_____

VEGGIE/TUNA NOODLE BAKE

1 can vegetable soup
1/3 to 1/2 cup skim milk
1 can (7 ounces water packed) tuna, drained & flaked
2 cups cooked EGGLESS noodles
1 tablespoon chopped parsley
3 slices tomato, cut in half

METHOD:
Empty soup into bowl.
Gradually blend in skim milk.
Mix in tuna, EGGLESS noodles and parsley.
Spoon into shallow baking dish.
Top with tomato.
Bake at 350 degrees for 20 minutes.

SERVES: 4

FATS PER SERVING: 3

Notes: _____

_____

_____

_____

Rating For This Recipe	
❏ Poor	❏ Fair
❏ Good	❏ Excellent

ZESTY CHICKEN CASSEROLE

Preheat oven to 350 degrees.
1 broiler/fryer (about 3 pounds) cooked, without skin,
and deboned.
Place broth in refrigerator and skim off all fat.
Strain and place in large stew pot.
Cook 12 ounces of THIN spaghetti in the broth then drain.
Set aside. Save the broth

1 cup onion, chopped
2 cups celery, chopped
2 cans famous brand tomatoes with green chilies,
drained and chopped.
1 can cream of mushroom soup
1 cup skim milk

METHOD:
Stir all of the ingredients together and
place in a sprayed casserole dish.
Bake 30 minutes, or until bubbling.
When combining ingredients, if it looks a little dry, add some
of the saved broth to the casserole ingredients.

SERVES: 8

FATS PER SERVING: 6

Rating For This Recipe
❑ Poor   ❑ Fair
❑ Good   ❑ Excellent

Notes: _____
_____
_____
_____

Notes: _____

_____

_____

_____

Rating For This Recipe	
❏ Poor	❏ Fair
❏ Good	❏ Excellent

DESSERTS:

APPLE CAKE

1 package LITE yellow cake mix
6 ounces egg substitute
1 can LITE apple pie filling

METHOD:
Beat eggs in mixing bowl.
Add cake mix and pie filling.
Beat well.
Pour into jelly roll pan 15 1/2 x 10 1/2 x 1-inch.
Sprinkle following on top:
1/3 cup brown sugar
1 tablespoon flour
1 tablespoon famous brand FAT FREE margarine
1 teaspoon cinnamon
Blend sugar, flour, margarine and cinnamon with fingers.
Top cake.
Bake at 350 degrees for 30 minutes.

SERVES: 8

FATS PER SERVING: TRACE

Rating For This Recipe
❑ Poor ❑ Fair
❑ Good ❑ Excellent

Notes: _____
_____
_____
_____

APPLESAUCE CAKE

2 1/2 cups flour
2 tablespoons shortening
4-ounce carton egg substitute
1 1/2 cups sugar
1/2 teaspoon salt
1/2 teaspoon soda
1/4 teaspoon cloves
1 1/3 cups thick unsweetened applesauce
1 teaspoon baking powder
1 cup raisins

METHOD:
Cream shortening and sugar.
Add eggs and beat well.
Add applesauce alternately with dry ingredients which have
been sifted together.
Beat until smooth.
Add raisins.
Spray a 9 x 13 baking pan with a non-stick cooking spray,
then lightly flour the pan.
Bake 40 to 60 minutes in 350-degree oven.

SERVES: 8

FATS PER SERVING: 4

Notes: _____
_____
_____
_____

Rating For This Recipe
❏ Poor ❏ Fair
❏ Good ❏ Excellent

APPLE CAKE PUDDING

8 tablespoons famous brand FAT FREE margarine
1 cup sugar
1 teaspoon soda
1/2 teaspoon salt
4 ounces egg substitute
1 teaspoon cinnamon
1 cup flour
1 teaspoon nutmeg
2 cups chopped apples (peeled)
1 cup dry raisins

METHOD:
Sift together the dry ingredients.
Cream margarine, sugar, and egg.
Add dry ingredients to creamed mixture. Mix well.
Add apples (thinly sliced) and raisins.
Grease baking pan 8 x 8 x 2-inch and spread mixture
(which is thick) in pan.
Bake in 350-degree oven for 1 hour.
Remove from oven and sprinkle with powdered sugar.

SERVES: 9-12

FATS PER SERVING: TRACE

Rating For This Recipe
❑ Poor   ❑ Fair
❑ Good   ❑ Excellent

Notes: _____

_____

_____

_____

BAKED PEARS

2 pounds Bosc or Bartlett pears
2 tablespoons sugar
1 teaspoon ground cinnamon
2 tablespoons lemon juice
1/2 cup water
1/4 teaspoon FAT FREE margarine

METHOD:
Preheat oven to 325 degrees.
Wash, pare and core, then halve pears.
Arrange cut side down in sprayed shallow baking dish.
Sprinkle with sugar, cinnamon and lemon juice.
Mix margarine in water and pour around pears.
Cover dish and bake for 45-60 minutes, depending on
type of pears used, or until fork tender.

SERVES: 4-5

FATS PER SERVING: FAT FREE

Notes: _____

_____

_____

_____

Rating For This Recipe	
❏ Poor	❏ Fair
❏ Good	❏ Excellent

BLACKBERRY JAM CAKE

2 cups sugar
1 cup LOW FAT buttermilk
1 teaspoon baking powder
1 tablespoon cinnamon
10 ounces egg substitute
2 cups blackberry jam
1 cup famous brand FAT FREE margarine
4 cups flour
1 teaspoon soda
1/2 teaspoon allspice

METHOD:
Cream sugar; add margarine, then buttermilk.
Sift the flour, soda, baking powder and spices.
Add to the mixture.
Then add jam.
Put egg substitute in last.
Grease and flour four 8-inch cake pans.
Bake until toothpick inserted in middle is clean.
Bake in moderate oven (350 degrees).
This makes a 4-layer cake.

SERVES: 8

FATS PER SERVING: 1
WATCH THOSE CALORIES!

Rating For This Recipe
❑ Poor ❑ Fair
❑ Good ❑ Excellent

Notes: _____
_____
_____
_____

BOILED ICING

1 1/2 cups sugar, divided
3/4 cup water
1 tablespoon light corn syrup
2 egg whites
1/8 teaspoon salt
1 teaspoon vanilla

METHOD:
Reserve 2 tablespoon of the sugar.
Combine remaining sugar with water and corn syrup in
a heavy saucepan.
Cook over medium heat stirring constantly until sugar
dissolves and syrup is clear.
Cook without stirring to soft ball stage (240 degrees).
Remove from heat.
Quickly beat egg whites and salt until soft peaks form,
gradually adding reserved sugar.
Beat until blended.
Continue to beat, slowly adding syrup mix. Add vanilla
and beat until stiff peaks form and frosting is thick.

YIELDS 4 cups frosting

FATS PER SERVING: FAT FREE

Notes: _____

_____

_____

_____

Rating For This Recipe
❏ Poor   ❏ Fair
❏ Good   ❏ Excellent

CHOCOLATE ZUCCHINI CAKE

Preheat oven to 350 degrees
2 cups flour (unsifted)
1 teaspoon baking powder
1 teaspoon soda
1/4 teaspoon salt
1 teaspoon cinnamon
1/4 cup cocoa
3/4 cup egg substitute
1 1/2 cup sugar
3/4 cup LOW FAT buttermilk
1/2 cup applesauce
2 cups shredded zucchini
1 teaspoon vanilla
1/2 cup raisins

METHOD:
Spray and flour 10-inch bundt pan.
Sift dry ingredients EXCEPT sugar and set aside.
In a large mixing bowl, beat egg substitute and sugar
until light and fluffy, adding sugar slowly.
Add applesauce, milk and dry ingredients alternately
until well-blended.
Fold in zucchini and vanilla and raisins.
Pour in prepared pan.
Bake 55-60 minutes or until it tests done.
Cool on wire rack 10 minutes, then remove from pan.
SERVES: 16

FATS PER SERVING: TRACE

Rating For This Recipe
❑ Poor ❑ Fair
❑ Good ❑ Excellent

Notes: _____
_____
_____
_____

COCOA PUDDING CAKE

1 cup all purpose flour
3/4 cup sugar
2 tablespoons cocoa powder
2 teaspoons baking powder
1/2 teaspoon salt
1/2 cup skim milk
1 1/2 tablespoons honey
1 teaspoon vanilla
non-stick cooking spray
3/4 cup brown sugar
1/4 cup cocoa powder
1 3/4 cups hot water

"WATCH THOSE CALORIES!"

METHOD:
Sift together flour, sugar, 2 tablespoons cocoa,
baking powder and salt.
Add the milk, honey and vanilla, mixing by hand until smooth.
Spray an 8-inch square pan with non-stick spray.
Pour batter into the pan.
Combine the brown sugar, 1/4 cup cocoa and water.
Pour over the batter.
Bake at 350 degrees for 45 minutes

SERVES: 8

FATS PER SERVING: 1
WATCH THOSE CALORIES!

Notes: _____
_____
_____
_____

Rating For This Recipe
❑ Poor ❑ Fair
❑ Good ❑ Excellent

COTTON PICKIN' CAKE

1 box LITE yellow cake mix, mixed
according to directions but using
3/4 cup egg substitutes to replace the 3 called-for eggs.
1 can mandarin oranges, drained and cut up

METHOD:
Mix cake and add chopped mandarin oranges
Bake according to package directions. Let cake
cool completely.

Frost with:
4-ounce FAT FREE cream cheese
Small can drained crushed pineapple
Small tub lite whipped topping
Small box vanilla instant pudding, dry

METHOD:
Mix frosting ingredients well and ice cake.

SERVES: 12-16

FATS PER SERVING: 2

Rating For This Recipe
❏ Poor ❏ Fair
❏ Good ❏ Excellent

Notes: _____
_____
_____
_____

DIETER'S PIE CRUST

1/3 cup sifted all-purpose flour
1/8 teaspoon salt
2 tablespoons shortening
1/2 cup FAT FREE cottage cheese

METHOD:
Use a cloth to squeeze cottage cheese dry.
Then sieve. Discard liquid.
Cut shortening into dry ingredients as for regular pie crust.
Add the cottage cheese, mixing lightly with a fork until a
ball of dough is formed.
Turn out on very light floured pastry cloth & roll to fit
8" or 9" pie pan.
For a baked pie shell, bake at 400 degrees for 20 minutes.

SERVES: 6

FATS PER SERVING: 5

Notes: _____

_____

_____

_____

Rating For This Recipe	
❏ Poor	❏ Fair
❏ Good	❏ Excellent

DOODLE CAKE

2 cups flour
2 cups sugar
4 ounces egg substitute
1 teaspoon soda
2 cups crushed pineapple (juice included)

METHOD:
Combine ingredients in large mixing bowl and beat until
well-blended.
Pour into a greased and floured pan, 9 x 12 x 2-inch.
Bake in 350-degree oven for 30-40 minutes.

Frosting for Cake:
1 8-ounce package FAT FREE cream cheese
4 tablespoons famous brand FAT FREE margarine
1 cup brown sugar
Cream margarine and cream cheese.
Beat in sugar.
Ice cake while still hot.

SERVES: 9-12

FATS PER SERVING: TRACE

Rating For This Recipe
❑ Poor ❑ Fair
❑ Good ❑ Excellent

Notes: _____
_____
_____
_____

"EASY CUSTARD PIE" (Makes own crust)

8 ounces egg substitute
1/8 teaspoon nutmeg (or to taste)
1/2 cup sugar
2 heaping tablespoons flour
1/8 teaspoon salt
2 cups skim milk

METHOD:
To slightly beaten eggs add sugar, salt, nutmeg and flour.
Stir in milk.
Grease a 9-inch pie plate with famous brand FAT FREE
margarine, and pour in.
Sprinkle top with nutmeg if desired.
Bake 375 - 400 degrees 30 minutes or until firm.

SERVES: 6

FATS PER SERVING: TRACE

Notes: _____

_____

_____

_____

Rating For This Recipe	
❏ Poor	❏ Fair
❏ Good	❏ Excellent

EASY PINEAPPLE PIE

1 large can crushed pineapple in own juice
1 package SUGAR FREE lemon instant pudding and pie filling
1 cup skim milk
1 small carton LITE whipped topping
2 tablespoons real lemon reconstituted lemon juice
OR fresh lemon juice
1 teaspoon lemon peel, grated (optional)

METHOD:
Drain pineapple well.
Combine pudding mix and milk in medium bowl.
Beat 2-3 minutes until very thick.
Fold in whipped topping, pineapple, lemon juice and peel.
Pour into a prepared crust.
Refrigerate 4 hours or overnight.
Garnish with squiggle of lite whipped topping if desired.

NOTE:
Spray pie pan with a non-stick butter-flavored spray.
Crush 9 LOW FAT graham crackers.
Pat down on bottom of pie plate.
This will help filling set.

SERVES: 6

FATS PER SERVING: TRACE

Rating For This Recipe
❑ Poor ❑ Fair
❑ Good ❑ Excellent

Notes: _____

_____

_____

_____

FAT FREE BREAD PUDDING

1/4 cup egg substitute
3 cups skim milk
1 tablespoon vanilla
1/2 cup raisins
1/3 cup plus 2 tablespoons sugar
12-14 slices day-old FAT FREE bread

METHOD:
Tear bread into bite-sized pieces and place in a 9 x 13 baking
dish that has been sprayed with butter-flavored cooking spray.
Mix egg substitute and skim milk together in a saucepan and
heat to boiling with the sugar, stirring constantly.
Remove from heat and add raisins.   Let sit 5 minutes.
While waiting, preheat oven to 350 degrees, pour milk mixture
over bread and place in oven. Bake 45 minutes or so.
Serve warm or cold.

May use the following as a sauce.
In a saucepan, mix together:
1/3 cup sugar
1/8 teaspoon salt
1 tablespoon cornstarch
Slowly add:
1 cup water
Cook until thick. Then add:
1/4 teaspoon famous brand FAT FREE margarine
1 1/2 teaspoons vanilla
1/2 teaspoon cinnamon
1/4 teaspoon nutmeg
SERVES: 9-12

FATS PER SERVING: FAT FREE

Notes: _____

_____

_____

_____

Rating For This Recipe
❏ Poor   ❏ Fair
❏ Good   ❏ Excellent

FAT FREE CHEESECAKE

1 Small package SUGAR FREE gelatin
lemon or lime flavor
Juice of 1 lemon or lime (about 1 tablespoon)
2/3 cup boiling water
1 cup FAT FREE cottage cheese
1 8-ounce container FAT FREE cream cheese
2 cups lite whipped topping - prepared with skim milk
1 cup reduced calorie cherry pie filling
(Optional)

METHOD:
Spray 9-inch pie plate with non-stick cooking spray.
Completely dissolve gelatin in boiling water.
Add fruit juice and stir well.
Pour into a blender container.
Add cheeses and blend at medium speed for 2
minutes, scraping sides occasionally.
Blend until smooth.
Pour into a large bowl and fold in the lite whipped topping.
Pour into prepared pan and smooth top.
Chill until set.
Just before serving, you may add the
pie filling to the top of the lemon cheesecake.
(I suggest doubling recipe and pour in spring form pan for a
thicker cheese cake.)

SERVES: 8

FATS PER SERVING: FAT FREE

Rating For This Recipe	Notes: _____
❏ Poor ❏ Fair	_____
❏ Good ❏ Excellent	_____

FAT FREE CHOCOLATE SAUCE

3/4 cup sugar
1/3 cup unsweetened cocoa powder
4 teaspoons cornstarch
2/3 cup evaporated skim milk
1 teaspoon vanilla

METHOD:
In a small saucepan, combine all of the dry ingredients.
Slowly add the milk.
Cook and stir over medium heat until thickened and bubbly.
Cook and stir 2 minutes more.
Remove from heat and stir in vanilla.
Serve warm or cold.
May use over ice cream, yogurt or angel food cake
and fresh fruit.
May keep leftover sauce in a covered container
in the refrigerator for up to 1 week.

Makes 1 cup

FATS PER SERVING: FAT FREE

Notes: _____
_____
_____
_____

Rating For This Recipe
❏ Poor ❏ Fair
❏ Good ❏ Excellent

FAT FREE GRAHAM CRACKER CRUST

1 1/2 cups crushed LOW FAT graham crackers
1/4 cup famous brand FAT FREE margarine

METHOD:
Crush enough crackers to measure 1 1/2 cups.
Stir in the margarine.
Mix well and press into bottom and up sides of
a 9-inch pie plate.
Bake about 10 minutes in 400-degree oven.
For an extra "FAT FREE margarine" flavor, spray
with butter-flavored non-stick cooking spray
prior to baking.

SERVES: 6-8

FATS PER SERVING: LOW FAT
WATCH THOSE CALORIES!

"Have you joined LFC yet?"

Rating For This Recipe	
❏ Poor	❏ Fair
❏ Good	❏ Excellent

Notes: _____

_____

_____

_____

FRESH PEACH PIE

3/4 cup sugar
2 1/2 tablespoons cornstarch
1/2 teaspoon cinnamon
6 cups fresh peaches, sliced
1 tablespoon famous brand FAT FREE margarine
1 tablespoon lemon juice

METHOD:
Mix sugar, cornstarch, cinnamon and a dash of salt together.
Pour over peaches and sprinkle with lemon juice.
Toss together.
Pour into unbaked pastry shell.
(See crust receipt on page 68)
Dot with FAT FREE margarine.
Bake about 40 minutes in a 425-degree oven.

SERVES: 6

FATS PER SERVING: FAT FREE

Notes: _____

_____

_____

_____

Rating For This Recipe
❑ Poor   ❑ Fair
❑ Good   ❑ Excellent

FUDGE MARBLE POUND CAKE

Preheat oven to 350 degrees.
1 box famous brand fudge marble cake mix
1 package SUGAR FREE vanilla instant pudding mix
(4-serving size)
8-ounce carton egg substitute (equivalent to cake directions.
i.e. 4 ounces = 2 eggs; 8 ounces equal 4 eggs.)
1 cup water
3 tablespoons vegetable oil
spray and flour two 9 x 5 x 3 loaf pans.

METHOD:
Lay cocoa packet from cake mix aside. Combine cake mix,
pudding mix, egg substitutes, water and oil in a large bowl.
Beat at medium speed on mixer for 2 minutes.
Measure out 1 cup of the batter and place in a small bowl.
Stir in cocoa packet.
Spoon 1/2 the yellow batter in each pan,
then 1/2 of the chocolate on top of it.
Run knife around through the batters to marble.
Bake for 45-50 minutes or until toothpick comes out clean.
Cool in pans for 5 minutes.
Loosen and invert onto a cooling rack.
Cool completely, then slice loaf into 18 equal 1/2-inch slices.
Freeze 2nd loaf.

Makes 2 loaves: 18 slices each.

FATS PER SERVING: 3

Rating For This Recipe
❏ Poor ❏ Fair
❏ Good ❏ Excellent

Notes: _____

_____

_____

_____

FUDGY BROWNIES

1/4 cup applesauce
1/2 cup sugar
1 teaspoon vanilla
1/2 cup all purpose flour
2 tablespoons unsweetened cocoa
1/4 cup egg substitute
1/2 cup firmly packed light brown sugar

METHOD:
In a large bowl combine sugars, flour, cocoa, applesauce
and egg substitute until well-blended.
Stir in vanilla.
Spread batter evenly in a well-sprayed
8 x 8 x 2 inch baking pan.
Bake at 350 degrees for 30 minutes or until done.
Cool in pan on wire rack.
Cut into 2-inch squares while warm.
These will be very moist, but
assume a brownie texture as they cool.

SERVES: 16

FATS PER SERVING: 2

Notes: _____

_____

_____

_____

Rating For This Recipe
❑ Poor ❑ Fair
❑ Good ❑ Excellent

HOMEMADE ICE CREAM

Dissolve 2 packs unflavored gelatin in
1/2 cup cold water to soften
Stir in 1/2 cup HOT water

Mix together:
4 13-1/2-ounce cans evaporated skim milk
12 packs sweetener
1 tablespoon real vanilla
1 teaspoon lemon extract (optional)

METHOD:
Combine all of the ingredients in the freezer can
and set up freezer according to manufacturer's instructions.
Crank until firm.
1 1/2 cups fresh diced fruit of your choice may be added
before freezing, if desired.
(Note) This is a very low-caloried, FAT FREE dessert.
It is also very tasty.
You may top it with the chocolate sauce.

SERVES: 6-8

FATS PER SERVING: FAT FREE

Rating For This Recipe
❏ Poor ❏ Fair
❏ Good ❏ Excellent

Notes: _____
_____
_____
_____

ICE BOX CAKE

1 small box SUGAR FREE strawberry or cherry gelatin
1 box LITE whipped topping made according to package
directions using skim milk
12 vanilla wafers

METHOD:
Mix gelatin according to package directions and
chill until slightly thickened.
Beat with an electric mixer until light and foamy.
Fold into the lite whipped topping.
Place cookies in bottom of 8 x 8 x 2 cake pan.
Pour gelatin mix over the cookies.
Chill.

SERVES: 8

FATS PER SERVING: 1

Notes: _____

_____

_____

_____

Rating For This Recipe
❑ Poor ❑ Fair
❑ Good ❑ Excellent

LEAN DREAM

Dissolve:
1 small package SUGAR FREE lemon or lime gelatin in
1 cup boiling water
Add 1/2 pound marshmallows and stir until dissolved.

Add to gelatin mixture:
1 small package FAT FREE cream cheese
1 cup FAT FREE salad dressing
1 10-ounce can crushed pineapple
Place in refrigerator until beginning to congeal, then fold
in 1 cup lite whipped topping, which has been whipped stiff.
Place in large baking dish and let cool until firm.
Dissolve small package cherry gelatin in 2 cups boiling
water.
Cool.
When it begins to congeal, pour over salad and chill.
Serve with snack crackers.

SERVES: 6-8

FATS PER SERVING: FAT FREE

Rating For This Recipe
❑ Poor ❑ Fair
❑ Good ❑ Excellent

Notes: _____
_____
_____
_____

LO-CAL WATERGATE DESSERT

1 can crushed pineapple, drained
1 box SUGAR FREE pistaschio pudding
1 package LITE dry whipped topping, mixed according to package directions, using skim milk

METHOD:
Mix dry pudding with drained pineapple and fold
into the prepared lite whipped topping.
Chill and serve.

SERVES: 4-6

FATS PER SERVING: FAT FREE and LO-CAL

Notes: _____

_____

_____

_____

Rating For This Recipe	
❏ Poor	❏ Fair
❏ Good	❏ Excellent

JAM CAKE

4 cups flour
2 cups sugar
1 teaspoon nutmeg
1 teaspoon cloves
1 cup famous brand FAT FREE margarine
2 teaspoons cinnamon
1 1/2 cups LOW FAT buttermilk
3 4-ounce cartons of egg substitute
2 teaspoons soda
2 cups blackberry jam
1 cup cherry preserves
1 cup crushed pineapple, drained

METHOD:
Mix dry ingredients.
Cream egg substitute and margarine.
Mix buttermilk and dry ingredients alternately.
Add to margarine and eggs.
Add: 2 cups blackberry jam
        1 cup cherry preserves
        1 cup crushed pineapple, drained
Bake at 350 degrees. Makes 3 layers.

SERVES: 8

FATS PER SERVING: 1

Rating For This Recipe
❏ Poor ❏ Fair
❏ Good ❏ Excellent

Notes: _____
_____
_____
_____

LO-CAL PUMPKIN PIE FILLING

2 cups pumpkin
2 tablespoons plus 2 teaspoons cornstarch
1 cup evaporated skim milk
1 envelope unflavored gelatin
1 teaspoon pumpkin pie spice
1 teaspoon cinnamon
2 teaspoon famous brand FAT FREE margarine
1 teaspoon vanilla
4 teaspoons brown sugar substitute

METHOD:
Mix cornstarch and milk thoroughly.
Add the remaining ingredients, EXCEPT the gelatin.
Cook over medium heat until thick.
Stir in the gelatin.
Pour into a baked pie shell (pie shell recipe on page 68).
Refrigerate until firm.

SERVES: 6

FATS PER SERVING: FAT FREE

Notes: _____
_____
_____
_____

Rating For This Recipe	
❏ Poor	❏ Fair
❏ Good	❏ Excellent

OLD FASHIONED RICE PUDDING

4 cups COLD skim milk
1 cup of instant rice
1 package SUGAR FREE vanilla pudding (not instant)
1/4 cup raisins (optional)
1/4 cup egg substitute
1/4 teaspoon ground cinnamon
1/8 teaspoon ground nutmeg

METHOD:
Combine milk, rice, pudding mix,
raisins and egg substitute in medium saucepan.
Bring to a full boil over medium heat, stirring constantly.
Remove from heat and cool 5 minutes, stirring twice.
Pour into individual dessert dishes or serving bowl.
Sprinkle with cinnamon and nutmeg.

SERVES: 4-6

FATS PER SERVING: TRACE

Rating For This Recipe
❑ Poor ❑ Fair
❑ Good ❑ Excellent

Notes: _____
_____
_____
_____

PARTY CAKE

Bake one box LITE yellow cake mix using lower
cholesterol method

Icing:
1 small package instant vanilla pudding
1 cup skim milk
1 8-ounce FAT FREE cream cheese
Maraschino cherries
9-ounce dry whipped topping prepared with skim milk
1 8-ounce can crushed pineapple

METHOD:
Dissolve instant vanilla pudding in milk
and set aside.
In large bowl, beat cream cheese until creamy.
Add lite whipped topping and beat with mixer.
Add pudding mixture and beat again.
Icing should be like whipped cream.
Ice cake.
Drain pineapple and spread on icing.
Place maraschino cherries on top.
Keep refrigerated.

SERVES: 8-10

FATS PER SERVING: TRACE

Notes: _____

_____

_____

_____

Rating For This Recipe
❑ Poor ❑ Fair
❑ Good ❑ Excellent

PASTRY FOR ONE CRUST PIE

1 cup sifted all-purpose flour
3/4 teaspoon salt
4 tablespoons LOW FAT margarine (stick)
2 tablespoons skim milk

METHOD:
Combine flour and salt in a bowl.
Combine the flour mixture and margarine, using a fork or pastry blender, until the texture is like coarse cornmeal.
Add the COLD milk, stirring until well-mixed.
Shape into a ball, place on a piece of waxed paper, flatten and cover with another sheet of waxed paper.
Dampen counter if necessary to keep waxed paper from slipping.
Roll out with a rolling pin to about a 10-inch circle.
Turn upside down over pie pan, peeling off papers.
Trim dough and flute edge.

IF DOUGH TEARS, DO NOT USE WATER TO REPAIR. MEND WITHOUT MOISTENING.

IF crust is to be baked before filling is added, prick all over with a fork and bake about 10 minutes.
Cool before adding filling.
IF filling the shell, follow filling directions.

SERVES: 6

FATS PER SERVING: 5

Rating For This Recipe
❏ Poor ❏ Fair
❏ Good ❏ Excellent

Notes: _____
_____
_____
_____

PINEAPPLE CHERRY CRUNCH

1 20-ounce can crushed pineapple, slightly drained
1 can LITE cherry pie filling
1 box LITE yellow or white cake mix (2 layer size)
1/4 cup melted famous brand FAT FREE margarine
1/2 cup grape nut cereal, optional

METHOD:
Put pineapple in bottom of a 9 x 13-inch pan.
Spoon cherry pie filling over top.
Spread dry cake mix next.
Pour melted margarine over dry cake mix.
Sprinkle grape nuts on top.
Bake at 350 degrees for 35-40 minutes or until top is brown.

SERVES: 6-8

FATS PER SERVING: TRACE

Notes: _____

_____

_____

_____

Rating For This Recipe	
❑ Poor	❑ Fair
❑ Good	❑ Excellent

PUMPKIN CUSTARD

2 cups pumpkin
3/4 cup sugar
1/2 teaspoon salt
2 teaspoons pumpkin pie spice
1 1/2 cup evaporated skim milk
4 ounces egg beaters
1 teaspoon vanilla

METHOD:
Preheat oven to 425 degrees.
Mix all of the above ingredients in a bowl until well-blended.
Pour into a prepared 9-inch pie pan with graham
cracker crust. (See page 75).
Bake in pre-heated oven at 425 degrees for 15 minutes.
Reduce heat to 350 degrees for 40-50 minutes.
Test whether it is done by inserting knife in center of pie.
If knife comes out clean, she's done!
Cool and chill.
Cut in wedges and serve with a dallop of LITE
whipped topping.

SERVES: 6

FATS PER SERVING: TRACE

Rating For This Recipe
❑ Poor ❑ Fair
❑ Good ❑ Excellent

Notes: _____
_____
_____
_____

RED VELVET LIGHT CAKE

1/2 cup FAT FREE, low-calorie margarine
4 ounces FAT FREE cream cheese
1 1/2 cups sugar
1/2 cup egg substitute
2 1-ounce bottles red food coloring
2 1/4 cups sifted cake flour
2 tablespoons unsweetened cocoa
1 teaspoon baking soda
1/4 teaspoon salt
1 cup LOW FAT buttermilk
1 teaspoon vanilla

METHOD:
Beat margarine and cream cheese at medium speed
with mixer until creamy.
Gradually add the sugar, beating well after each addition.
Stir egg substitute in food coloring
Gradually add egg substitute, beating after each addition.
Combine flour and next 3 ingredients; add to margarine
mixture alternately with buttermilk, beginning and ending
with flour.
Mix just until blended.
Pour batter into three 9-inch cake pans coated with
cooking spray.
Bake at 350 degrees for 18 minutes.
Cool in pans on wire rack.
Remove from pans and cool completely on racks.
Spread frosting (see page 64 for frosting directions)
between layers and over top and sides of cake.

SERVES: 16

FATS PER SERVING: 2

Notes: _____

_____

_____

_____

Rating For This Recipe
❑ Poor ❑ Fair
❑ Good ❑ Excellent

RIBBON DESSERT

1 cup sugar OR 4 packs sweetener (DO NOT USE EQUAL)
2 cups skim milk
2 packages unflavored gelatin
2 cups FAT FREE sour cream
2 teaspoons vanilla
1 3-ounce package each of SUGAR FREE lime, lemon,
orange and cherry gelatin

METHOD:
Spray a 9 x 13 glass dish with non-stick cooking spray.
Bring skim milk to a boil and add sugar OR sweetener.
Remove from heat and add gelatin that has been
dissolved in a small amount of water to the milk.
Place in a blender and add the sour cream and vanilla.
Blend for 2 minutes, scraping down sides.
Prepare the flavored gelatin, one box at a time,
using 1 cup of boiling water and 1/2 cup cold water.
Pour into the bottom of the glass dish, chill until set.
When firm, pour 1 1/2 cups of the sour cream mixture
on top and again chill until set.
Continue until all the flavors and sour cream mixture
have been layered.
Chill and cut into squares.
Serve with a dollop of lite whipped topping for a beautiful
lo-cal dessert.
SERVES: 8

FATS PER SERVING: FAT FREE

Rating For This Recipe
❏ Poor ❏ Fair
❏ Good ❏ Excellent

Notes: _____
_____
_____
_____

RHUBARB BERRY DELITE

4 cups diced rhubarb
2 cups fresh OR frozen strawberries
3/4 cup sugar
1 package SUGAR FREE strawberry or raspberry gelatin
2 cups boiling water
1 cup skim milk
1 envelope unflavored gelatin
1/4 cup cold water
1 1/2 teaspoons vanilla
2 cups FAT FREE sour cream

METHOD:
In a saucepan, cook rhubarb, strawberries and sugar until tender.
Dissolve gelatin in boiling water.
Stir enough packs of a sugar substitute to fruit that has cooled
slightly to sweeten to taste.
Stir into the gelatin mix.   Set aside.
In another pan, heat milk. Soften unflavored gelatin in cold water.
Add to hot milk and stir until gelatin dissolves.
Remove from heat and add vanilla.
Cool to lukewarm and blend in sour cream.
Set aside at room temperature.
Pour 1/3 of fruit mixture into a 3-quart bowl, chill until almost set.
Spoon a third of the sour cream mixture over the fruit and
chill until almost set.
Repeat twice, chilling between layers if necessary.
Refrigerate until firm. At least 3 hours.
SERVES: 12

FATS PER SERVING: FAT FREE

Notes: _____

_____

_____

_____

Rating For This Recipe
❑ Poor ❑ Fair
❑ Good ❑ Excellent

SENSATIONAL DOUBLE LAYER PUMPKIN PIE

1 cup FAT FREE cream cheese
1 tablespoon skim milk
1 tablespoon sugar
1 1/2 cups thawed LITE whipped topping
1 graham cracker pie crust
(SEE RECIPE for crust on page 75)
1 cup skim milk OR evaporated skim milk
2 packages SUGAR FREE vanilla instant pudding
1 16-ounce can of pumpkin
1 teaspoon ground cinnamon
1/2 teaspoon ground ginger
1/4 teaspoon ground cloves

METHOD:
Soften cream cheese and mix with the tablespoon milk and
sugar in a large bowl. Using a wire whisk, beat until smooth.
Gently stir in lite whipped topping and spread mixture on
bottom of crust.
Pour 1 cup milk into a bowl and add pudding mix.
Whisk until well blended, 1-2 minutes. (Mixture will be thick)
Stir in pumpkin and the spices using the whisk.
Spread over the cream cheese mixture.
Refrigerate at least 3 hours.
Garnish with more lite whipped topping if desired.
SERVES: 8
FATS PER SERVING: FAT FREE

Rating For This Recipe
❏ Poor   ❏ Fair
❏ Good   ❏ Excellent

Notes: _____

_____

_____

_____

STRAWBERRY CREAM ROLL

1 carton egg substitute
1 teaspoon vanilla
3/4 cup sugar
3/4 cup sifted cake flour
1 teaspoon baking powder
1/4 teaspoon salt
Confectioner's sugar

CREAM FILLING:
2 cups lite whipped topping made according to package
directions using skim milk
1 8-ounce container of FAT FREE cream cheese
1/4 cup confectioner's sugar
2 cups fresh or drained frozen strawberries cut up

METHOD:
Beat eggs with vanilla on high speed
with an electric mixer for 5 minutes.
Gradually add the sugar, beating until dissolved.
Combine flour, baking powder and salt and fold into
egg mixture until combined.
Line a jelly roll pan with wax paper and spray with
non-stick cooking spray.
Spread batter evenly in pan and bake in oven
at 375 degrees for 10-12 minutes.
Turn onto towel that has been sprinkled with powdered sugar.
Roll up after peeling off paper. Cool.   Unroll and fill with
cream filling then re-roll, chill at least 2 hours.

SERVES: 10

FATS PER SERVING: FAT FREE

Notes: _____

_____

_____

_____

Rating For This Recipe
❑ Poor ❑ Fair
❑ Good ❑ Excellent

STRAWBERRY CREAM DESSERT

2 packages unflavored gelatin OR
2 boxes SUGAR FREE strawberry gelatin
1 can diet strawberry soda
1 cup evaporated skim milk
1 teaspoon vanilla
2 cups sliced pineapple, in its own juice, drained
1 cup frozen strawberries
2 tablespoons pineapple juice
Sweetener to taste

METHOD:
Sprinkle gelatin (either one) over soda in a saucepan.
Heat until gelatin is dissolved.
In a blender, chop pineapple, add the evaporated
skim milk, pineapple juice and vanilla.
Blend until well-mixed.
Add frozen berries and sweetener and blend until the
consistency of whipped cream.
Add the cooled gelatin mixture and continue blending.
A WORD OF CAUTION...the mixture will almost come
out of the blender.
You may pour this dessert into a mold if desired, or
pour in a 9 x 13 pan. Chill for several hours.

SERVES: 6-8

FATS PER SERVING: FAT FREE

Rating For This Recipe	Notes: _____
❑ Poor ❑ Fair	_____
❑ Good ❑ Excellent	_____
	_____

STRAWBERRY JELLY

2 teaspoons unflavored gelatin
1 cup crushed strawberries
1/2 teaspoon of vanilla
LOW-CAL sweetener to equal 4 teaspoons of sugar

METHOD:
In a saucepan, sprinkle 2 teaspoons unflavored gelatin
over 3/4 cup cold water.
Cook over medium heat, stirring until gelatin dissolves.
Add:
1 cup crushed strawberries. Heat throughly.
Remove from heat and add:
1/2 teaspoon vanilla
sweetener to equal 4 teaspoons sugar.
Refrigerate.

MAKES about one pint

FATS PER SERVING: FAT FREE

Notes: _____

_____

_____

_____

Rating For This Recipe	
❑ Poor	❑ Fair
❑ Good	❑ Excellent

SURPRISE COBBLER

1 1/2 cups all-purpose flour
2 teaspoons baking powder
1/2 teaspoon salt
1/2 cup sugar minus 2 tablespoons
1 cup skim milk
3 or 4 cups of your favorite fruit
that has been sweetened with
1/2 cup sugar OR you may use a
large can of sliced peaches in their own juice, drained

METHOD:
Sift flour with salt, baking powder and sugar.
Add milk and beat until smooth.
Put into a 2-quart baking dish that has been
sprayed with butter-flavored cooking spray.
Put fruit in center.
Bake at 350 degrees for 40-50 minutes or
until a knife inserted in the center comes out clean.
Best when served warm with a dollop of lite whipped topping.

SERVES: 6

FATS PER SERVING: TRACE

Rating For This Recipe
❑ Poor   ❑ Fair
❑ Good   ❑ Excellent

Notes: _____

_____

_____

_____

STRAWBERRY TRIFLE

FOR VANILLA CUSTARD:
2 tablespoons cornstarch
1/4 cup granulated sugar
1 1/2 cups skim milk
1 1/2 tablespoons egg substitute
1 tablespoon famous brand NO FAT margarine
1 1/4 teaspoons REAL vanilla

METHOD:
Combine sugar and cornstarch in a heavy saucepan.
Whisk in milk until well blended.
Bring to a boil over medium heat, stirring often.
Boil, whisking, 30 seconds to cook cornstarch.
Remove from heat.
In a small bowl, whisk egg substitute, slowly adding 1 cup
of the hot mixture.
Whisk back into the remaining mixture and return to heat.
Cook over medium heat, whisking constantly for
30 seconds more.
Remove from heat and beat in margarine and vanilla.
Let stand until slightly cool, whisking several times.
Cover with a sheet of waxed paper and refrigerate
until cool.
Must be chilled to use with trifle (Continue "Trifle", p.99)

Notes: _____

_____

_____

_____

Rating For This Recipe
❏ Poor ❏ Fair
❏ Good ❏ Excellent

TRIFLE

2 pints fresh strawberries, hulled and halved
3-4 tablespoons sugar, depending on sweetness of berries.
1 1/2 tablespoons orange juice
1 small FAT FREE angel food cake
3 tablespoons LO CAL raspberry jam

METHOD:
In a medium sized bowl, combine the berries, sugar and juice.
Let stand at room temperature about 30 minutes, tossing
occasionally.
Cut the cake into 3 equal layers.
Spread 1/2 of the raspberry jam over the bottom layer.
Replace middle layer and cover with remaining jam.
Add top layer and cut the cake into 3/4-inch slices.

TO ASSEMBLE:
Line bottom and sides of a 1 1/2-quart glass
serving bowl with two-thirds of the jam-filled cake slices.
Drizzle about 1/4 cup juice from the berries over the cake.
Spoon 1/2 of the custard over the cake and spread 1/2 of
the strawberries over the custard.
Cover with remaining cake slices. Drizzle with remaining
berry juice and top with custard and berries.
Chill at least 6 hours before serving covering with plastic
wrap or lid.

SERVES: 6-8

FATS PER SERVING: FAT FREE

Rating For This Recipe
❏ Poor ❏ Fair
❏ Good ❏ Excellent

Notes: _____

_____

_____

_____

Notes: _____

_____

_____

_____

Rating For This Recipe
❏ Poor   ❏ Fair
❏ Good   ❏ Excellent

MEATS:

BEEF STROGANOFF

1 pound ground round
1 16-ounce package EGGLESS noodles, cooked and drained
8-ounce container FAT FREE sour cream
1/2 cup FAT FREE Miracle Whip
1 cup cream of mushroom soup
1 cup skim milk
1 onion, chopped

METHOD:
Spray skillet with a non-stick cooking spray and
brown ground meat and onion.
Drain well on paper towels when done.
Return meat to skillet that has been wiped clean.
Add rest of the ingredients and stir well to mix.
Cook on low heat until bubbly.
May also place cooked noodles on a plate and
cover with meat mixture and heat in microwave until hot.
Serve with a green salad for a complete meal.

SERVES: 8

FATS PER SERVING: 4

Rating For This Recipe
❑ Poor ❑ Fair
❑ Good ❑ Excellent

Notes: _____
_____
_____
_____

BISCUITS AND CHICKEN GRAVY

2 cups cooked, diced chicken breasts
1 10-ounce package frozen peas
1/2 cup cream of chicken soup
1 cup skim milk
1/2 cup FAT FREE sour cream
1/2 teaspoon salt
1/2 teaspoon pepper
1 1/4 cups shredded FAT FREE Cheddar cheese
1 can LOW FAT biscuits

METHOD:
Rinse peas under running water to separate.
Place in saucepan with rest of the ingredients, except
biscuits, and heat to boiling.
Pour into a sprayed casserole dish and top with biscuits.
Bake in a 425-degree oven for about 20 minutes, or
until biscuits are brown and casserole is bubbling.

SERVES: 6

FATS PER SERVING: 5

Notes: _____

_____

_____

_____

Rating For This Recipe	
❑ Poor	❑ Fair
❑ Good	❑ Excellent

CHICKEN KABOBS

4 3-ounce boneless skinned chicken breasts
1 can pineapple chunks, drained, reserving juice
1 green pepper, cut in 1-inch pieces
1 red pepper, cut in 1-inch pieces
1/2 cup teriayaki sauce
2 tablespoons brown sugar
Cherry tomatoes OR tomato chunks

METHOD:
Mix teriayaki sauce, and 1/4 cup of the reserved juice
and brown sugar together in a bowl.
Cut chicken breasts in chunks and add to marinade.
Refrigerate for at least 3 hours.
Thread chicken on skewer, alternating with pineapple,
pepper and tomato.
Zucchini or other vegetables may be added if desired.
Grill over medium coals 12-15 minutes, turning
often and basting with marinade.

SERVES: 4

FATS PER SERVING: 4

Rating For This Recipe
❏ Poor   ❏ Fair
❏ Good   ❏ Excellent

Notes: _____
_____
_____
_____

CHICKEN POT PIE

1 3-1/2 pound broiler/fryer, skinned
2 quarts water
1/2 teaspoon salt
1/2 teaspoon pepper
1 stalk celery, cut into 2-inch pieces
1 medium onion, quartered
1 bay leaf
3 1/2 cups peeled and cubed potatoes
1 16-ounce package frozen mixed vegetables
1 cup skim milk
1/2 cup all-purpose flour
3/4 teaspoon salt
1 teaspoon pepper
1/2 teaspoon poultry seasoning
5 sheets frozen phyllo pastry, thawed
Butter-flavored cooking spray

METHOD:
Combine first 7 ingredients in a large Dutch oven.
Bring to a boil, cover, then reduce heat and simmer 1 hour or until chicken is tender.
Remove the chicken reserving the broth but discarding the vegetables and bay leaf.
Cool, then bone chicken and cut into bite-size pieces.
Remove fat (oily liquid) from cooled broth.
Measure out 3 1/2 cups and return it to the Dutch oven.
Bring to a boil and add potatoes and mixed vegetables.
Return to a boil, then reduce heat. Cover and cook about 8 minutes, or until vegetables are tender.

Notes: _____
_____
_____
_____

Rating For This Recipe
❑ Poor ❑ Fair
❑ Good ❑ Excellent

CHICKEN POT PIE con't

Combine the milk and flour in a jar, cover tightly and
shake to mix.
Gradually add the milk mixture in a slow stream to the
broth mixture, stirring constantly.
Cook until thickened.
Stir in salt, pepper, poultry seasoning and chicken.
Spray 13 x 9 x 2 inch baking dish with butter-flavored
cooking spray.
Set aside after spooning in chicken mixture.
Place 1 phyllo sheet on a flat surface, keeping remaining
sheets covered with a damp towel to prevent drying until
ready to use.
Coat first sheet with butter-flavored cooking spray.
Layer remaining 4 sheets on first sheet,
coating each with butter-flavored cooking spray.
Place the 5 stacked sheets on top of the baking dish.
Loosely crush edges around the dish.
Bake at 400 degrees for 20 minutes.

SERVES: 8

FATS PER SERVING: 7

Rating For This Recipe
❑ Poor ❑ Fair
❑ Good ❑ Excellent

Notes: _____
_____
_____
_____

DOWN-HOME CREOLE DINNER

(Chicken and Sausage Jambalaya)

4 4-ounce skinned, boned chicken breast halves
1 pound LEAN turkey sausage (I perfer Mr. Turkey brand, chopped)
1/4 teaspoon ground red pepper
1/4 teaspoon ground black pepper
1/2 teaspoon creole seasoning (I added this)
Vegetable cooking spray
2 1/4 cups chopped onion
2 cups chopped celery
1 1/2 cups sliced green onions
1/2 cup chopped green pepper
1/2 cup chopped sweet red pepper
2 cloves garlic, minced
2 1/2 cups water
1 teaspoon chicken-flavored bouillon granules
(I deboned the chicken and boiled the bones in
2 1/2 cups water and substituted the broth for the
water and bouillon granules above.)
1/2 teaspoon browning and seasoning sauce, optional
1 1/4 cups long-grain rice, uncooked

METHOD:
Cut chicken into bite-size pieces; sprinkle with ground
red and black pepper and creole seasoning.
Spray LARGE electric skillet or wok with
non-stick vegetable cooking spray.
Add chicken and cook 3 to 5 minutes.

Notes: _____
_____
_____
_____

Rating For This Recipe	
❏ Poor	❏ Fair
❏ Good	❏ Excellent

DOWN-HOME CREOLE DINNER cont'd

Remove chicken; drain and pat dry with paper towel.
Add sausage; cook approximately 3 minutes.
Remove, drain and pat dry.
Add onion and next 5 ingredients; sauté until tender.
Return chicken and sausage to skillet.
Add water, bouillon, browning and seasoning sauce and rice.
Bring to a boil.
Cover, reduce heat and simmer 20 minutes or until rice
is tender and liquid is absorbed.
Spoon Jambalaya into individual bowls;
garnish with green onion fans, if desired.
Serve with a salad for a "Down-Home-Creole Dinner" —
Louisiana style.

SERVES: 6

FATS PER SERVING: 6

Rating For This Recipe	Notes: _____
❑ Poor   ❑ Fair
❑ Good   ❑ Excellent

DYNAMO CHICKEN TACOS

1 cup onion, chopped
1 clove garlic, minced
2 cups cooked, chopped chicken breasts
1 8-ounce can tomato sauce
1 4-ounce can chopped chili peppers, drained
12 FAT FREE flour tortillas
2 medium tomatoes, chopped and seeded
2 cups shredded lettuce
3/4 cup FAT FREE shredded Cheddar cheese

METHOD:
Spray preheated skillet with non-stick cooking spray.
Add garlic and onion and cook until tender.
Stir in chicken, tomato sauce and the chili peppers.
Cook until heated through.
Meanwhile, wrap the
tortillas in foil and heat in a 300-degree oven.
Heat thoroughly.
Divide the chicken mixture among the 12 tortillas.
Top with lettuce, tomatoes, and cheese.

SERVES: 12

FATS PER SERVING: 2

Notes: _____

_____

_____

_____

Rating For This Recipe
❑ Poor   ❑ Fair
❑ Good   ❑ Excellent

FRIED PORK CHOPS

4 3-ounce trimmed, LEAN pork chops
1 1/2 cups crushed FAT FREE cracker crumbs
1/4 cup egg substitute (equals 1 egg)
Seasoned salt (about 1 teaspoon)
Pepper to taste

METHOD:
Preheat and generously spray a non-stick skillet with
cooking spray.
Dip each chop in egg substitute and dip in finely
crushed cracker crumbs that have the seasoned
salt and pepper mixed in.
Place coated chops in the skillet, lower heat to low and cover.
Cook about 20 minutes, remove lid and turn.
Raise heat and brown on both sides.
Keep pouring off accumulated grease during cooking.

(see page 110 for gravy recipe)

SERVES: 4

FATS PER SERVING: 12

Rating For This Recipe
❑ Poor ❑ Fair
❑ Good ❑ Excellent

Notes: _____
_____
_____
_____

FRIED CHICKEN

1 3-pound broiler/fryer, cut up and skinned
1 8-ounce carton FAT FREE plain yogurt
1 1/2 cups FAT FREE Italian dried and seasoned
bread crumbs
Salt and pepper to taste

METHOD:
Preheat and spray a non-stick skillet.
Dip skinned chicken in the yogurt, then roll in
the seasoned crumbs.
Place chicken in the skillet and cook on low heat until
chicken is tender and juices are clear.
Cook covered.
Uncover and turn chicken at least twice during cooking.
When chicken is tender, raise heat and continue to cook,
uncovered, to allow the chicken to brown.
When chicken is done, remove from skillet and keep warm.
FOR GRAVY:
Scrape skillet to loosen crumbs.
Add about 1 tablespoon flour to skillet and stir.
Add skim milk to skillet and continue to stir, cooking
gravy until thickened to desired consistency.
Served with mashed potatoes and low-fat
biscuits for a "rib sticking menu!"

SERVES: 6

FATS PER SERVING: 11

Notes: _____

_____

_____

_____

Rating For This Recipe	
❏ Poor	❏ Fair
❏ Good	❏ Excellent

FRIED CHICKEN, LFC WAY

4 3-ounce chicken breasts
FAT FREE Italian season bread crumbs
Seasoned meat tenderizer
Paprika
Salt and pepper

METHOD:
Remove any skin from the chicken breast.
Wash in cold water.
Sprinkle with seasoned meat tenderizer, paprika,
salt and pepper.
Roll the chicken in the Italian seasoned bread crumbs.
Place in Teflon skillet on low heat.
Cook 50 minutes.
For the last ten minutes, turn heat up to brown.

SERVES: 4

FATS PER SERVING: 4

Rating For This Recipe	Notes: _____
❏ Poor ❏ Fair	_____
❏ Good ❏ Excellent	_____
	_____

GOOD MEAT SAUCE FOR SPAGHETTI

1 pound ground turkey breast
1/2 green pepper
1 clove garlic
1 small onion
1/2 teaspoon salt, pepper and celery salt
1 can tomato sauce
1 can tomato soup
2 teaspoons basil
2 teaspoons oregano
1/2 cup catsup
1/4 cup vinegar

METHOD:
Brown meat with pepper and onion.
Drain well.
Sprinkle with FAT FREE Parmesan cheese.
Add remaining ingredients and simmer 20-30 minutes.

SERVES: 6

FATS PER SERVING: 4

Notes: _____
_____
_____
_____

Rating For This Recipe
❏ Poor   ❏ Fair
❏ Good   ❏ Excellent

HAWAIIAN PORK CHOPS

4 3-ounce loin pork chops, trimmed and EXTRA LEAN
1/2 cup chopped onion
1/2 cup chopped green pepper
2 tablespoons flour
1 teaspoon salt
1/2 teaspoon pepper
6 slices pineapple, in own juice and drained, reserving juice
1 tablespoon vinegar
1/4 cup catsup
1/2 cup reserved pineapple juice

METHOD:
Spray a large, heavy skillet with non-stick cooking spray.
Cook onion and green pepper until onion is tender.
Remove from skillet.
Respray skillet.
Mix flour, salt and pepper and dredge pork chops.
Brown in skillet on both sides over medium heat.
Place pineapple slice on each chop, sprinkle onion
and green pepper over all.
Combine vinegar, catsup and pineapple juice to make
a sauce and pour over chops.
Cover and simmer over low heat for 45 minutes
or until chops are done.

SERVES: 4

FATS PER SERVING: 12

Notes: _____

Rating For This Recipe
❑ Poor ❑ Fair
❑ Good ❑ Excellent

_____
_____
_____

LEMON CHICKEN

4 3-ounce skinned and deboned chicken breasts,
pounded out thin
3/4 cup dry FAT FREE bread crumbs
1/4 cup egg substitute (equal to 1 egg)
1 clove garlic, crushed
1 lemon
1 teaspoon seasoned salt (or to taste)
Pepper to taste
1 cup NO FAT chicken broth, divided
1 1/2 tablespoons cornstarch stirred into
1/4 cup water

METHOD:
Sprinkle chicken breasts with seasoned salt and pepper.
In a preheated, sprayed non-stick skillet, sauté the
crushed garlic for 1 minute. Dip chicken breasts first into
the egg substitute then into the bread crumbs.
Arrange in the skillet and brown on both sides on low heat.
Cut the lemon in 1/2 and thinly slice and lay on top of chicken.
Squeeze the juice out of the second 1/2 lemon into the
1/2 cup of the broth and pour into the skillet. Cover.
Bring to a boil and reduce heat.
Cook until chicken is done.
Remove chicken from pan and keep warm.
SAUCE:
Add the reserved broth to the pan and stir to loosen crumbs
from skillet. Stir in cornstarch mixture and continue stirring
until thickened. Serve as a sauce over chicken.
SERVES: 4

Notes: _____

_____

_____

_____

Rating For This Recipe
❏ Poor ❏ Fair
❏ Good ❏ Excellent

MARINATED PORK CHOPS

6 3-ounce lean, boneless and trimmed pork chops
2 cups LOW sodium soy sauce
1 cup water
1/2 cup brown sugar substitute
1 teaspoon salt

METHOD:
Mix soy sauce, water, brown sugar
and salt thoroughly in a 13 x 9 pan.
Place chops in marinade and refrigerate overnight,
or at least 8 hours.
Bake at 350 degrees for 1 1/2 hours.

SERVES: 6

FATS PER SERVING: 9

Notes: _____

_____

_____

_____

MEATLOAF #1

1 1/2 pounds ground turkey breast
1 cup FAT FREE bread crumbs
1 medium onion
1 can famous brand tomato sauce
4 ounces egg substitute
1 1/2 teaspoons salt
1/4 teaspoon pepper

METHOD:
Mix all together and put in 350-degree oven.
Pour over topping basting about every 15 minutes.
1/2 can famous brand tomato sauce
1/2 cup water
2 tablespoons vinegar
2 tablespoons mustard
2 tablespoons brown sugar or molasses
Bake for about an hour.

SERVES: 6

FATS PER SERVING: 4

Notes: _____

_____

_____

_____

Rating For This Recipe	
❑ Poor	❑ Fair
❑ Good	❑ Excellent

MOM'S MEATLOAF

Preheat oven to 350 degrees

2 pounds ground round
2 egg whites
1 envelope dry onion soup & mushrooms
1 cup crushed FAT FREE crackers
1 teaspoon salt
1/4 teaspoon pepper
1/4 cup water
1 teaspoon Worcestershire sauce
1 grated carrot

METHOD:
Mix all ingredients EXCEPT water and form a loaf.
Place in a casserole dish and pour water around loaf.
Mix 1/3 cup catsup, 1 tablespoon vinegar,
1 tablespoon plus 1 teaspoon brown sugar.
Place on top of loaf.
Cover with foil.
Bake 1 hour or until done.

SERVES: 8

FATS PER SERVING: 5

Rating For This Recipe
❏ Poor ❏ Fair
❏ Good ❏ Excellent

Notes: _____
_____
_____
_____

OLD FASHIONED SLOPPY JOES

1 pound ground turkey breast
1/4 cup chopped onions
1/2 cup catsup
1/4 cup water
2 tablespoons celery
1 teaspoon lemon juice
1 1/2 teaspoons sugar
3/4 teaspoon Worcestershire sauce
1/2 teaspoon vinegar
3/4 teaspoon salt
1/8 teaspoon dry mustard

METHOD:
Brown onion and turkey.
Drain grease.
Add remaining ingredients.
Simmer covered for 30 minutes.

SERVES: 6

FATS PER SERVING: 3

Notes: _____

_____

_____

_____

Rating For This Recipe
❑ Poor ❑ Fair
❑ Good ❑ Excellent

PARMESAN CHICKEN

4 3-ounce chicken breasts, skinned and boned
2 cups soft FAT FREE bread crumbs
1/3 cup grated famous weight-loss brand
FAT FREE Parmesan cheese
1/4 cup fresh parsley
2 cloves garlic, minced
1 8-ounce carton FAT FREE plain yogurt

METHOD:
Mix bread crumbs, Parmesan cheese, parsley and garlic.
Dip chicken breasts in yogurt,
then into the mixed ingredients.
Place in a sprayed casserole and bake at 350 degrees
for 45-50 minutes.

SERVES: 4

FATS PER SERVING: 4

Rating For This Recipe	Notes: _____
❑ Poor ❑ Fair	_____
❑ Good ❑ Excellent	_____

"PLUM DELICIOUS" BAKED HAM

1 3-to-5 pound 95% FAT FREE, fully cooked boneless ham
2 jars plum baby food dessert (junior size) for glaze

METHOD:
Line 9 x 13 baking dish with heavy-duty foil.
Place rack in pan and put ham on it.
Bake in a slow, 200-degree oven.
for about 4 hours to heat through.
Cover ham with the plum "glaze" and bake 1/2 hour more,
adding "glaze" as a baste.

SERVES: 8-10

FATS PER SERVING: 8 per 4-ounce

Notes: _____

_____

_____

_____

Rating For This Recipe	
❑ Poor	❑ Fair
❑ Good	❑ Excellent

ROAST TURKEY

Preheat oven to 350 degrees.
8-pound young turkey
2 tablespoons lemon juice
1 teaspoon salt
1/8 teaspoon each of thyme and rosemary
1 cup celery tops
1 peeled onion
6 sprigs of parsley
3/4 cup FAT FREE chicken broth

METHOD:
Wash and pat dry turkey, inside and out, with paper towels.
Discard any excess fat.
Sprinkle cavity of the bird with lemon juice and rub
remaining juice into the skin.
Sprinkle the bird's cavity with the herbs and salt and fill
with the vegetables.
Truss the bird and rub 1/2 teaspoon salt into the skin.
Bake on a rack in a sprayed shallow roaster covered with
a loose foil tent.
Bake 2 hours.
Remove foil tent and baste with FAT FREE broth.
Continue baking 30 minutes more or until leg moves freely
(180 degrees if using a meat thermometer.)
Let sit 5 or more minutes, open cavity and discard vegetables.
Carve, discarding skin.

SERVES: 15

FATS PER SERVING: 9

Rating For This Recipe
❑ Poor ❑ Fair
❑ Good ❑ Excellent

Notes: _____

_____

_____

_____

SAVORY BURGER STEW

1 pound ground turkey breast
1 teaspoon instant onion flakes
1/4 teaspoon salt
1/8 teaspoon pepper
16-ounce can Veg-All vegetables, drained
10 1/2-ounce can tomato soup

METHOD:
Brown turkey and onion.
Drain; add seasonings.
Stir in Veg-All and soup.
Pour into 1 1/4-quart casserole dish.
Bake at 400 degrees for 15 minutes.
Serve with refrigerated biscuits or instant mashed potatoes.

SERVES: 4

FATS PER SERVING: 5

"Ride the LOWFAT WAVE of Healthy Eating."

Notes: _____

_____

_____

_____

Rating For This Recipe	
❑ Poor	❑ Fair
❑ Good	❑ Excellent

SHRIMP OR CHICKEN QUICHE IN A RICE CRUST

1/4 cup egg substitute (equals 1 egg)
2 cups cooked rice
2 ounces shredded FAT FREE Cheddar cheese

TO MAKE RICE CRUST:
Spray a 9-inch pie pan with non-stick spray.
Mix above ingredients thoroughly and press in bottom and up the sides of pie pan.
Bake at 425 degrees for 20-25 minutes or until lightly browned.
REDUCE HEAT TO 350 DEGREES

1 cup each green pepper and onion, chopped
1 garlic clove, minced
8 ounces cooked, deveined shrimp or cooked chicken.
3/4 cup egg substitute beaten (equals 3 eggs)
2 ounces (about 1/2 cup) shredded FAT FREE Cheddar cheese
1 tablespoon chopped parsley

METHOD:
Sauté vegetables until tender in a sprayed skillet.
Stir in rest of ingredients and pour into baked rice crust.
Return to 350-degree oven and bake 30-35 minutes or until set.
Let stand 5 minutes before cutting.

SERVES: 4

FATS PER SERVING: TRACE for shrimp OR 3 for chicken

Rating For This Recipe
❏ Poor ❏ Fair
❏ Good ❏ Excellent

Notes: _____

_____

_____

_____

SKILLETBURGER SUPPER

1 pound ground round
1 1/2 cups chopped onion
1 1/2 cups chopped celery
1 can tomato soup
1 1/2 tablespoons bottled barbecue sauce
1 teaspoon salt
1/2 teaspoon pepper

METHOD:
Brown and drain ground meat.
Add onion and celery.
Cook until tender but not browned,
then add remaining ingredients.
Cover and simmer for 30 minutes.
Serve on toasted FAT FREE buns.

SERVES: 8

FATS PER SERVING: 3

Notes: _____

_____

_____

_____

Rating For This Recipe	
❏ Poor	❏ Fair
❏ Good	❏ Excellent

SPICY PORK CHOPS

2 3-ounce LEAN pork chops
1 to 3 tablespoons chili powder
1 teaspoon salt
1/4 teaspoon ginger
1/4 teaspoon thyme
1/4 teaspoon pepper

METHOD:
Combine the first five ingredients
and rub over the pork chops.
Cover and refrigerate for 2-4 hours.
Grill over hot coals for 15 minutes per side or until juices
run clear OR until the internal temperature
reaches 160 degrees on a meat thermometer.

SERVES: 2

FATS PER SERVING: 12

Rating For This Recipe
❑ Poor ❑ Fair
❑ Good ❑ Excellent

Notes: _____
_____
_____
_____

SOUPER BURGERS

1 pound ground round
1 envelope dry onion soup mix
Salt and pepper to taste
1 tablespoon Worcestershire sauce

METHOD:
Mix all ingredients in a bowl and
pat into four 1/4-pound patties.
Grill over medium coals or broil to desired doneness.

SERVES: 4

FAT PER SERVING: 5

Notes: _____

_____

_____

_____

Rating For This Recipe	
❏ Poor	❏ Fair
❏ Good	❏ Excellent

SUNDAY BEST CHICKEN BREAST

Preheat oven to 350 degrees.

4 3-ounce chicken breasts.
Seasoned salt
Pepper to taste

METHOD:
Spray a baking pan with butter-flavored cooking spray.
Arrange chicken in pan and season
with seasoned salt and pepper.
Add enough water to be about 1/4-inch depending on
thickness and number of chicken breasts.
Cover with foil.
Bake 1 hour or until chicken is done.

GRAVY:
Defat broth in pan and thicken with cornstarch for a
delicious gravy.
Refrigerate extra chicken for use in stir fry,
salads or recipe calling for cooked chicken.

SERVES: 4

FATS PER SERVING: 4

Rating For This Recipe
❑ Poor ❑ Fair
❑ Good ❑ Excellent

Notes: _____
_____
_____
_____

SWEDISH MEATBALLS

1 pound ground round OR turkey breast
1 cup fine FAT FREE bread crumbs
1/4 cup egg substitute (equals 1 egg)
1/2 cup skim milk
1/2 can cream of mushroom soup
1 teaspoon salt
1/2 teaspoon pepper
1/2 teaspoon nutmeg
1/2 cup shredded FAT FREE Cheddar cheese

METHOD:
Mix all of the above ingredients EXCEPT cheese
and roll into 1-inch balls.
Broil on broiler pan until done
(about 5 minutes each side).
Place in a casserole dish.
Cover with 1/2 can cream of mushroom soup
diluted with 1/2 cup skim milk.
Bake at 325 degrees for 20 minutes covered.
Remove lid, sprinkle with 1/2 cup FAT FREE
Cheddar cheese.
Continue baking for 10-15 more minutes.

SERVES: 6

FATS PER SERVING: 5-3

Notes: _____
_____
_____
_____

Rating For This Recipe
❏ Poor ❏ Fair
❏ Good ❏ Excellent

SWEET & SOUR TURKEY MEATBALLS

1 pound ground turkey breast
1 tablespoon cornstarch
1 1/2 tablespoons chopped onion
2 ounces egg substitute
1/4 teaspoon salt
Dash pepper

METHOD:
Mix all together and form into 18 meatballs.
Fry until brown, drain well.
Put into casserole dish and cover with sauce.

Sauce:
1 large green pepper sliced or diced
1/3 cup pineapple juice
3 tablespoons cornstarch
1/2 cup mild vinegar
2/3 cup FAT FREE bouillon or chicken broth
1 tablespoon shortening
1 cup chunk pineapple
1 tablespoon soy sauce
2 tablespoons sugar
Sauté green pepper and pineapple
Mix cornstarch with juice and add to pepper and pineapple.
Mix other ingredients and pour over meatballs.

SERVES: 6

FATS PER SERVING: 3

Rating For This Recipe
❏ Poor ❏ Fair
❏ Good ❏ Excellent

Notes: _____

_____

_____

_____

TACO BURGERS

2 pounds ground round OR turkey breast
1 package taco seasoning mix
1 teaspoon salt
1/2 teaspoon pepper
1/2 cup ketchup

METHOD:
Mix all ingredients in a large bowl.
Make 8 large patties.
Grill or broil about 5 inches from heat.
Serve on FAT FREE buns, topping with chopped lettuce,
chopped tomatoes and shredded FAT FREE
Cheddar cheese.

SERVES: 8

FATS PER SERVING: 5-4

Notes: _____

_____

_____

_____

Rating For This Recipe	
❑ Poor	❑ Fair
❑ Good	❑ Excellent

VEGETABLE MEAT PIE

Preheat oven to 350 degrees.

1 pound ground round
1 cup famous brand bran Chex cereal crushed
1/4 cup egg substitute OR 1 egg white
1/2 cup catsup
1 teaspoon salt
1 teaspoon onion powder
1/4 teaspoon pepper
1/2 teaspoon chili powder
1 10-ounce package frozen mixed vegetables,
cooked and drained

METHOD:
Mix all of the above ingredients
together and let sit for 5 minutes.
Press gently into sprayed 9-inch pie plate or
casserole dish.
Bake uncovered about 30 minutes.
Let stand 5 or 10 minutes before serving.

SERVES: 8

FATS PER SERVING: 3

Rating For This Recipe
❏ Poor   ❏ Fair
❏ Good   ❏ Excellent

Notes: _____
_____
_____
_____

V.I.P. MEATLOAF

3 pounds ground round
1 cup sweet pickle relish
1 cup quick cooking oats
2 egg whites
1 medium onion, chopped
1 green pepper, chopped
1 cup tomato juice
1 cup FAT FREE cream cheese
Salt and pepper

METHOD:
Mix all ingredients.
Put into dish and bake for 1 1/4 hours at 350 degrees.

Topping:
3 tablespoons brown sugar substitute
1/4 cup catsup
1 teaspoon dry mustard
1/4 teaspoon nutmeg
Mix and pour over meatloaf.
Bake at 350 degrees.

SERVES: 8

FATS PER SERVING: 8

Notes: _____

_____

_____

_____

Rating For This Recipe
❑ Poor ❑ Fair
❑ Good ❑ Excellent

PASTA & GRAINS:

APPLE PANCAKES

1 cup flour
1/2 teaspoon salt
2 teaspoons sugar
1/4 cup egg substitute OR 1 egg white
1 cup skim milk
2 teaspoons vegetable oil
5 medium-size apples, peeled and thinly sliced

METHOD:
Combine milk, egg substitues (or egg whites) and oil.
Add to dry ingredients that have been blended in a small bowl.
Fold in apples.
Pour batter into a sprayed Teflon skillet and
spread to a 5-inch circle.
Turn when bubbles form and cook second side until
golden brown and apples are tender.

Makes 14 pancakes.

FATS PER SERVING: 2 per pancake

Rating For This Recipe	Notes: _____
☐ Poor ☐ Fair	_____
☐ Good ☐ Excellent	_____
	_____

BAKED PANCAKES

Preheat oven to 450 degrees.
3/4 cup egg substitute (equals 3 eggs)
1/2 teaspoon salt
1/2 cup flour
1/2 cup skim milk

METHOD:
In a mixing bowl, beat the egg substitute until light and fluffy.
Add salt, flour and milk.
Beat well.
Pour into a heavy skillet that has been sprayed with
butter-flavored cooking spray.
Bake 15 minutes, then reduce heat to 350 degrees and
bake 5 minutes more.
Remove to a platter and sprinkle with powdered sugar.
Good for Sunday brunch with fresh fruit or melon.

SERVES: 4-6

FATS PER SERVING: FAT FREE

Notes: _____

_____

_____

_____

Rating For This Recipe	
❏ Poor	❏ Fair
❏ Good	❏ Excellent

BANANA BREAD MIX

4 ounces FAT FREE cream cheese
5 medium over-ripe bananas
8 ounces egg substitute
Add 1 box LITE yellow cake mix.

METHOD:
Beat until well blended.
Bake at 350 degrees.
Loaf – bake 35 to 40 minutes;
Cake – bake 30 to 35 minutes.

Makes two large loaf pans or one 9 x 13 cake.

FATS PER SERVING: TRACE

Rating For This Recipe
☐ Poor ☐ Fair
☐ Good ☐ Excellent

Notes: _____
_____
_____
_____

CHICKEN BROCCOLI FETTUCINI

1 tablespoon famous brand FAT FREE margarine
1 clove garlic, minced
1 can (10 3/4-ounce) broccoli cheese soup
1 cup skim milk
1/4 cup grated famous weight-loss brand FAT FREE
Parmesan cheese
1 1/2 cups cooked chicken cut in strips
3 cups hot cooked FAT FREE noddles (8 ounce dry)

METHOD:
In skillet, in hot margarine, cook garlic 2 minutes,
stirring constantly.
Stir in soup, milk and cheese.
Heat to boiling.
Add chicken.
Cook over low heat; 5 minutes, stirring often.
Toss with fettucini.
Garnish with cherry tomatoes and fresh parsley if desired.

SERVES: 4

FATS PER SERVING: 6

Notes: _____

_____

_____

_____

Rating For This Recipe
☐ Poor ☐ Fair
☐ Good ☐ Excellent

CHILI PASTA GRANDE

1/4 cup chopped green pepper
1/2 cup chopped onion
1 16-ounce can tomatoes, chopped
1 15-ounce can kidney beans, rinsed and drained
1 jalapeno pepper chopped (about 1 tablespoon)
2 teaspoons chili powder
1/4 teaspoon ground cumin
8 ounces elbow macaroni cooked and drained
1/2 cup FAT FREE sour cream

METHOD:
In a preheated sprayed skillet,
sauté onion and pepper about 2 minutes.
Add tomatoes and their juice, beans, jalapeno and chili
powder and cumin.
Bring to a boil, reduce heat and simmer about 15 minutes,
stirring occasionally.
Toss with cooked macaroni,
garnish with sour cream if desired.
Serve with cornbread and a salad.   Ole!

SERVES: 6

FATS PER SERVING: 1

Rating For This Recipe
☐ Poor ☐ Fair
☐ Good ☐ Excellent

Notes: _____
_____
_____
_____

CRANBERRY BREAD

2 cups flour
1 cup sugar
1 1/2 teaspoons baking powder
1/2 teaspoon soda
1 teaspoon salt
1/4 cup applesauce
3/4 cup orange juice
4 ounces egg substitute
1 cup cranberries, chopped

METHOD:

Sift dry ingredients and mix in applesauce until mixture
resembles coarse cornmeal.
Combine orange juice with egg substitute.
Pour all at once into dry ingredients mixing just enough
to dampen.
Carefully fold in cranberries.
Pour carefully into sprayed loaf pan.
Spread corners and sides slightly higher than center.
Bake 350 degrees for 1 hour.
Cool overnight before slicing.

Makes one loaf

FATS PER SERVING: TRACE

Notes: _____

_____

_____

_____

Rating For This Recipe	
❑ Poor	❑ Fair
❑ Good	❑ Excellent

FAT FREE CORNBREAD

2 cups SELF-RISING yellow cornmeal
1/4 cup honey
1 egg white OR 1/4 cup egg substitute
1 cup skim milk

METHOD:
Mix the above ingredients until well-moistened.
Spray 9-inch pan or muffin tin with non-stick cooking spray.
Bake in 425-degree oven about 15 minutes for muffins
and 15-20 minutes for cake pan.

SERVES: 6-8

FATS PER SERVING: TRACE

Rating For This Recipe	Notes: _____
☐ Poor ☐ Fair	_____
☐ Good ☐ Excellent	_____
	_____

ENGLISH MUFFIN BREAD

5 cups flour
2 packages active dry yeast
1 tablespoon sugar
2 teaspoons salt
1/4 teaspoon baking soda
2 cups warm (120 degrees) skim milk
1/2 cup warm (120-30 degrees) water
Cornmeal

METHOD:
Combine 2 cups flour, yeast, sugar, salt and baking soda
in a large bowl. Add warm milk and water, beat on low
speed for 30 seconds, scraping bowl occasionally.
Beat on high speed for 3 minutes.
Stir in remaining flour. Batter will be stiff.
DO NOT KNEAD.
Divide batter between two sprayed loaf pans.
sprinkled with cornmeal.
Spoon the batter into the pans and sprinkle cornmeal on top.
Cover and let rise in a warm place until doubled.
About 45 minutes.
Bake at 375 degrees for 35 minutes or until golden brown.
Remove from pans immediately and let cool on a rack.
Makes 2 loaves.
Freezes well. MAKES one loaf

SERVES: 14

FATS PER SERVING: TRACE

Notes: _____

_____

_____

_____

Rating For This Recipe
❑ Poor ❑ Fair
❑ Good ❑ Excellent

FRENCH TOAST

1/2 cup egg substitute
2 tablespoons skim milk
1 teaspoon sugar
1/8 teaspoon cinnamon
4 slices FAT FREE bread

METHOD:
Mix egg substitute, milk, sugar and cinnamon in pie pan.
Spray skillet with butter-flavored non-stick cooking spray
and preheat.
Dip bread in mixture and place in skillet.
Brown on one side and turn and brown on other side.
Serve with Low-Calorie pancake syrup.

SERVES: 2

FATS PER SERVING: FAT FREE

Rating For This Recipe	Notes: _____
☐ Poor ☐ Fair	_____
☐ Good ☐ Excellent	_____

LAMB LOVERS NOODLE STROGANOFF

2 pounds ground LEAN lamb
2 garlic cloves, minced
1 16-ounce can tomato sauce
1 teaspoon salt
1/4 teaspoon pepper
1 16-ounce pack EGGLESS noodles, cooked & drained
1 8-ounce carton FAT FREE cream cheese
1 16-ounce container FAT FREE sour cream
6 green onions
1 1/2 cups shredded FAT FREE Cheddar cheese
Paprika

METHOD:
Broil ground lamb on a broiler pan until done.
Drain well and pat out on a paper towel to remove excess fat.
Place lamb in a sauce pan that has been sprayed with
with non-stick cooking spray, sprinkle salt and pepper
on lamb, then simmer uncovered for 10 minutes.
Place drained noodles in a sprayed 13 X 9 baking dish.
Top with meat mixture.
In a small bowl, beat FAT FREE sour cream and cream
cheese until smooth.
Add onions and spread over meat mixture.
Sprinkle with cheese.
Bake 30 minutes at 350 degrees.
Sprinkle with paprika.

SERVES: 8-10

FATS PER SERVING: 15

Notes: _____

_____

_____

_____

Rating For This Recipe
❑ Poor ❑ Fair
❑ Good ❑ Excellent

LASAGNA

1 pound ground round
1 1/2 tablespoons garlic powder
1 tablespoon parsley
1 tablespoon sweet basil
1 1/2 teaspoons salt
2 cups tomatoes
2 16-ounce cans tomato paste
10 ounces lasagna noodles
3 cups FAT FREE cottage cheese
1/2 cup egg substitute (equal to 2 eggs)
1/2 teaspoon pepper
2 tablespoons parsley
1/4 cup famous weight-loss brand FAT FREE Parmesan cheese
1/2 pound FAT FREE shredded Mozzarella cheese

METHOD:
Brown and drain meat.
Add next 6 ingredients, simmer uncovered 30 minutes,
stirring occasionally.
Cook noodles in salt water, drain and rinse.
Mix cottage cheese, egg substitute, seasonings and
Parmesan cheese.
Layer noodles, 1/2 the Mozzarella cheese and 1/2 the meat
mixture.
Repeat layers, topping with the Mozzarella cheese.
Bake for 30 minutes at 375 degrees.
SERVES: 8

FATS PER SERVING: 3

Rating For This Recipe
☐ Poor ☐ Fair
☐ Good ☐ Excellent

Notes: _____
_____
_____
_____

LASAGNA CASSEROLE

Preheat oven to 375 degrees.
1 pound ground round
1 pound can tomatoes
3 8-ounce cans tomato sauce
1/2 cup onion
1/4 cup green pepper
1 1/2 teaspoons salt
1/4 teaspoon pepper
1/3 teaspoon oregano
10-ounces lasagna noodles, cooked and drained
1 12-ounce package FAT FREE Mozzarella cheese

METHOD:
Brown and drain ground meat.
Add tomatoes, tomato sauce, onion, green peppers,
oregano, salt and pepper.
Simmer about 1 hour,
Spoon 1/4 of the sauce into a 13 x 9 x 2 baking dish that
has been sprayed with a non-stick cooking spray.
Arrange a layer of noodles over sauce and sprinkle
half the cheese over them.
Repeat layers.
Bake for 30-45 minutes.
Allow to stand 5 minutes before serving.

SERVES: 8

FATS PER SERVING: 3

Notes: _____

_____

_____

_____

Rating For This Recipe	
❑ Poor	❑ Fair
❑ Good	❑ Excellent

MEXICAN CORN BREAD

1 cup all-purpose cornmeal
8 ounces egg substitute
1 cup skim milk
1/2 teaspoon soda
1 teaspoon salt
1/2 cup applesauce
1/2 pound FAT FREE grated cheese
2 jalapeno peppers
1 chopped onion
Garlic

METHOD:
Mix ingredients except cheese and peppers.
Pour half of batter into skillet, cover with cheese and
peppers, pour on rest of batter.
Bake 45 minutes in a 350-degree oven.

SERVES: 6

FATS PER SERVING: TRACE

Rating For This Recipe	Notes: _____
☐ Poor ☐ Fair	_____
☐ Good ☐ Excellent	_____
	_____

RED BEANS AND RICE

4 15- OR 16-ounce cans red beans drained and washed
1 16-ounce (1 pound) turkey sausage (I prefer Mr. Turkey brand)
1 large bell pepper, chopped
2 garlic cloves, minced
1 cup celery, chopped
2 medium onions, chopped
1 tablespoon chili powder
1/2 teaspoons basil leaves or 2 bay leaves
Pinch of oregano
Pinch of thyme
Salt and pepper to taste

METHOD:
Put 3 cans of red beans in Crock-Pot (save the fourth can to
be used later).
Cut sausage crosswise into 1/2- to 3/4-inch pieces and add.
Turn Crock-Pot to high until beans and sausage begin to cook.
Add chopped vegetables and spices.
Add salt and pepper to taste.
The amount needed will depend on spices in sausage and on
your own taste.   Add 1/2 cup water.
Turn Crock-Pot to low and let mixture cook for 8 hours.
About 1 hour before end of cooking time, mash the fourth can
of red beans and add to Crock-Pot to thicken soup.
Continue cooking mixture until tender.
Serve over fluffy rice with garlic bread and green salad.
Garnish with crushed red pepper or chopped Jalapeno peppers
(optional) or hot sauce.

SERVES: 8

FATS PER SERVING: 2

Notes: _____
_____
_____
_____

Rating For This Recipe
❏ Poor ❏ Fair
❏ Good ❏ Excellent

SAGE DRESSING

4 cups of crumbled corn bread. See recipe on page 139.
2 cups FAT FREE chicken broth.
2 cups diced celery
2 cups diced onion
3 teaspoons (or more) dried sage
2 teaspoons salt
1 teaspoon pepper
2 egg whites
1 small peeled apple diced

METHOD:
Cook onion and celery in 1 1/2 cups water until tender;
then drain
In a large mixing bowl, combine vegetables, bread,
and seasonings.
Slowly add chicken broth, using enough to thoroughly
moisten bread.
Stir in egg whites and if needed, more broth.
Pour into a baking dish that has been sprayed with
butter-flavored cooking spray.
Smooth evenly in dish.
Bake 30-40 minutes in a 350 degree oven until nicely
brown on top.

SERVES: 6-8

FATS PER SERVING: FAT FREE

Rating For This Recipe	Notes: _____
☐ Poor ☐ Fair	_____
☐ Good ☐ Excellent	_____

SALMON PATTIES

1 can of salmon
FAT FREE crackers
2 egg whites (discard yokes)

METHOD:
Mix salmon as you normally would to fry.
Substitute with FAT FREE crackers.
Add 2 egg whites.
Use a Teflon skillet and spray with non-stick cooking spray.
Cook on low heat till done.
Turn heat up at end of cooking time in order to brown.

SERVES: 4

FATS PER SERVING: 4

Notes: _____

_____

_____

_____

Rating For This Recipe	
❑ Poor	❑ Fair
❑ Good	❑ Excellent

STRAWBERRY BREAD

1 cup famous brand FAT FREE margarine
1 1/2 cups sugar
1 teaspoon vanilla
8 ounces egg substitute
3 cups flour
1 teaspoon salt
1 teaspoon cream of tartar
1 cup strawberry preserves
1/2 cup FAT FREE sour cream

METHOD:
Cream butter, sugar and vanilla.
Add egg substitute beating in.
Mix dry ingredients together.
Mix preserves and sour cream and add alternately with the
flour mixture, then add to first mixture.
If you really want pink bread, use a few drops of coloring.
Apricot preserves can be substituted if you like.
Bake 350 degrees till done.
Can be frozen.

Makes 1 large loaf or 6 small cans can be used.

FATS PER SERVING: TRACE

Rating For This Recipe	Notes: _____
☐ Poor ☐ Fair	_____
☐ Good ☐ Excellent	_____
	_____

TUNA FRITTERS

1 cup of flour
1 teaspoon salt
1 teaspoon baking powder
1/2 cup egg substitute (equals 2 eggs)
1/4 cup skim milk
1 large can tuna packed in spring water, drained and flaked
1 tablespoon dried onion flakes

METHOD:
Sift flour, baking powder and salt into mixing bowl.
Add egg substitute and milk.
Stir until all the flour is moistened.
Add tuna and onion flakes.
Spray a preheated skillet with non-stick cooking spray
and drop batter by the spoonful forming a circle about 3
inches across.
Cook over low heat until browned.
Respray skillet and brown other side.

SERVES: 6

FATS PER SERVING: TRACE

Notes: _____
_____
_____
_____

Rating For This Recipe
❑ Poor ❑ Fair
❑ Good ❑ Excellent

VEGETABLE ROTINI

1 can (10 3/4 ounce) FAT FREE broccoli cheese soup
1 package (3 ounce) FAT FREE cream cheese, softened
3/4 cup skim milk
2 tablespoons Dijon-style mustard (optional)
1/8 teaspoon pepper
3 cups cooked rotini (corkscrew) macaroni
(about 1 1/2 cups dry)
3 cups cooked precut fresh vegetables (broccoli flowerets,
cauliflowerets, carrots). If desire, substitute 1 bag
(16 ounce) any frozen vegetable combination, cooked and
drained for fresh vegetables.
1/2 cup grated FAT FREE Parmesan cheese

METHOD:
In 3-quart saucepan, gradually stir soup into cream cheese.
Add milk, mustard and pepper.
Cook over low heat, stirring often.
Add macaroni, vegetables and Parmesan cheese.
Heat throughly, stirring often.

SERVES: 4

FATS PER SERVING: 2

BROCCOLI
CHEESE

| Rating For This Recipe |
| Poor ☐ Fair ☐ |
| Good ☐ Excellent ☐ |

Notes: _____
_____
_____
_____

WING DING MUFFINS

Preheat oven to 375 degrees.
1 can low-fat biscuits
1 pound ground round
1/2 cup catsup
3 tablespoons brown sugar substitute
1 tablespoon vinegar
1 teaspoon chili powder
1 cup shredded FAT FREE Cheddar cheese

METHOD:
Spray muffin tin with non-stick cooking spray. Set aside.
Separate biscuits and pat out
on flat surface into 5-inch rounds.
Press in the bottom and up the sides of muffin cup.
Set aside.
Brown the meat, drain well on paper towels
and return to skillet.
In a small bowl, mix catsup, brown sugar, vinegar and chili
powder, stirring until smooth.
Add to the meat and mix well.
Divide the mixture among the biscuit-lined
muffin cups, then sprinkle each with cheese.
Bake 18-20 minutes or until golden brown.
Cool about 5 minutes before removing from the tin.
Serve with a hearty green salad.
SERVES: 10

FATS PER SERVING: 3

Notes: _____

_____

_____

_____

Rating For This Recipe
❏ Poor   ❏ Fair
❏ Good   ❏ Excellent

ZUCCHINI BREAD

6 ounces egg substitute
1 cup sugar plus 1 cup sugar substitute (I prefer Sugar Twin)
3 teaspoons vanilla
1 cup applesauce
2 cups shredded zucchini

METHOD:
Mix above ingredients.

Add:
3 cups flour
1/2 teaspoon baking powder
1 teaspoon salt
1 teaspoon baking soda
3 teaspoons cinnamon
3/4 cups of raisins

Pour mix into 2 loaf pans.
Bake 45 minutes to 1 hour at 350 degrees.

Makes 2 loaves.

FATS PER SERVING: FAT FREE

Notes: _____

_____

_____

_____

Rating For This Recipe
❑ Poor ❑ Fair
❑ Good ❑ Excellent

Notes: _____

_____

_____

_____

Rating For This Recipe	
❏ Poor	❏ Fair
❏ Good	❏ Excellent

SALADS

APRICOT GEL SALAD

2 small boxes SUGAR FREE apricot gelatin
2 cups boiling water
1 1/2 cups cold water
1 can crushed pineapple in its own juice (drain and reserve juice)
2 bananas, sliced
40 miniature marshmallows

METHOD:
Mix gelatin with boiling water until dissolved.
Add cold water and stir.
Add pineapple, bananas, and marshmallows.
Mix well and allow to sit until firm.
Top with: Drained pineapple juice
1/8 teaspoon butter flavoring
1/4 cup sugar
2 tablespoons flour
2 ounces egg substitute (equals 1 egg)
1 8-ounce package FAT FREE cream cheese

METHOD:
Mix sugar and flour in a saucepan. Slowly stir in the juice. Add butter flavoring and egg substitute. Cook over medium heat until thickened, stirring constantly. Remove from stove and add FAT FREE cream cheese and stir until creamy and smooth. Cool, then spread over the gelatin mixture. Chill.
PREPARE: 1 package dry whipped topping according to package directions using skim milk. Spread over chilled salad/dessert.
SERVES: 9-12

FATS PER SERVING: FAT FREE

Notes: _____

Rating For This Recipe
❑ Poor ❑ Fair
❑ Good ❑ Excellent

_____
_____
_____
_____

BEET SALAD

1 small box SUGAR FREE lemon gelatin
1 can shoestring beets or whole ones cut to size
1 tablespoon vinegar

METHOD:
Pour liquid off beets and mix with water to make 2 cups.
Bring to boiling point and add to gelatin.
Add vinegar and beets.

SERVES: 6

FATS PER SERVING: FAT FREE

Notes: _____
_____
_____
_____

Rating For This Recipe	
❑ Poor	❑ Fair
❑ Good	❑ Excellent

BLUEBERRY SALAD

2 cups boiling water
2 small boxes SUGAR FREE blackberry gelatin
1 15-ounce can crushed pineapple
1 can LITE blueberry pie filling
Topping:
1/3 cup sugar
8 ounces FAT FREE cream cheese
1 carton FAT FREE sour cream

METHOD:
Dissolve gelatin in boiling water.
Add pineapple, undrained.
Add pie filling.
Let gel.
Top with topping mixed above as given.
Refrigerate until ready to serve.

SERVES: 6-8

FATS PER SERVING: FAT FREE

Notes: _____
_____
_____
_____

BUBBLY GREEN SALAD

1 3-ounce package SUGAR FREE lime gelatin
1 cup boiling water
1 cup DIET famous brand name lemon-lime soda
1 tablespoon sugar
1 teaspoon vanilla
1 8-ounce package FAT FREE cream cheese
1 can crushed pineapple, drained

METHOD:
In a blender, add gelatin that has been dissolved in the
boiling water, soda and the cream cheese.
Blend until smooth.
Add sugar and vanilla.
Stir in pineapple and a few drops of green food coloring.
Chill. Serve on lettuce.

SERVES: 9-12

FATS PER SERVING: FAT FREE

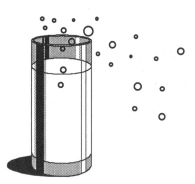

Notes: _____

_____

_____

_____

Rating For This Recipe	
❏ Poor	❏ Fair
❏ Good	❏ Excellent

CAULIFLOWER SALAD

1 small head of cauliflower, drained and coarsely chopped
2 stalks diced celery
1/2 green pepper chopped fine
1/2 teaspoon salt
1 dill pickle chopped
1 carrot grated
2 or 3 tablespoons chopped onion

METHOD:
Mix the above ingredients well and
Moisten with:
1/2 cup FAT FREE Miracle Whip or mayonnaise
1 packet sweetener
1 teaspoon prepared mustard.

SERVES: 4

FATS PER SERVING: FAT FREE

Notes: _____
_____
_____
_____

CINNAMON GEL SALAD

1/4 cup cinnamon candy (Red Hots)
1 1/2 cups hot water
1 (3 ounce) package SUGAR FREE cherry gelatin
1 cup chopped apples
1 cup chopped celery

METHOD:
Dissolve gelatin and Red Hots in hot water.
Let cool.
Add apples and celery.
Refrigerate.

SERVES: 6-8

FATS PER SERVING: FAT FREE

Notes: _____

_____

_____

_____

Rating For This Recipe	
❏ Poor	❏ Fair
❏ Good	❏ Excellent

COMPANY'S COMING FRUIT SALAD

3 bananas, sliced
1 small can mandarin oranges, well-drained
1 medium apple, chopped
1 medium can pineapple, well-drained
1 small bunch seedless grapes
1 small package instant SUGAR FREE lemon pudding mix
4 fresh peaches, sliced

METHOD:
Put fruit in bowl.
Mix all together.
Sprinkle instant lemon pudding mix over fruit (dry).
Mix well.
You can use fresh or well-drained canned fruit,
whichever you prefer.
Use 1/2 box dry pudding mix for medium-sized bowl.
For a large bowl, use the whole box.

SERVES: 6-8

FATS PER SERVING: FAT FREE

Rating For This Recipe
❑ Poor ❑ Fair
❑ Good ❑ Excellent

Notes: _____
_____
_____
_____

CRANBERRY PINEAPPLE TREAT

1 6-ounce package SUGAR FREE cherry gelatin mix
2 cups boiling water
1 16-ounce can whole cranberry sauce
2 cups drained, crushed pineapple, in its own juice,
reserving juice.
1 1/2 cups reserved juice, adding water if necessary.

METHOD:
Dissolve gelatin in boiling water.
Mix in the whole cranberry sauce, blending well.
Add the pineapple juice and mix well.
Chill until slightly thickened and add pineapple.
Chill until firm.

SERVES: 12

FATS PER SERVING: FAT FREE

Notes: _____
_____
_____
_____

Rating For This Recipe	
❑ Poor	❑ Fair
❑ Good	❑ Excellent

EASY LOW FAT FRUIT SALAD

1 can (21 ounce) LITE peach pie filling
3 bananas, sliced
2 cups fresh strawberries, sliced
1 cup seedless grapes

METHOD:
Combine all ingredients in a bowl
and chill several hours to blend flavors.

SERVES: 6-8

FATS PER SERVING: TRACE

Rating For This Recipe
❑ Poor ❑ Fair
❑ Good ❑ Excellent

Notes: _____

_____

_____

_____

FRESH FRUIT BOWL

8 or 10 cups fresh melon cubes
1-2 tablespoons white corn syrup
1 pint of fresh strawberries, hulled
2 cups fresh pineapple chunks
2 oranges, sectioned

METHOD:
In a large bowl, combine melon and corn syrup.
Cover and refrigerate overnight.
Just before serving stir in remaining fruit.
Garnish with fresh mint leaves if desired.

SERVES: 12-16

FATS PER SERVING: FAT FREE

Notes: _____

_____

_____

_____

Rating For This Recipe	
❏ Poor	❏ Fair
❏ Good	❏ Excellent

FRUIT SALAD FAT FREE:

1 can pineapple in juice
1 can large peaches drained
10-ounce strawberries in juice frozen, unsweetened
4 bananas
1 small package instant SUGAR FREE vanilla pudding (dry)
2 tablespoons famous orange drink mix (I prefer Tang)

METHOD:
Mix all together in a large bowl.
Great to serve over FAT FREE vanilla yogurt to make a
sundae.
It's also good as a fruit salad.

SERVES: 12-16

FATS PER SERVING: FAT FREE

"Have you heard of LFC?"

"Yes. You get to eat real food!"

Rating For This Recipe
❏ Poor ❏ Fair
❏ Good ❏ Excellent

Notes: _____
_____
_____
_____

FROZEN SOUR CREAM SALAD

1/2 cup sugar
2 cups FAT FREE sour cream
1 9-ounce can crushed pineapple (drained)
3 bananas
1/2 cup raisins, optional
1/4 cup maraschino cherries, optional

METHOD:
Mix all ingredients and freeze in baking cups in muffin tin.

SERVES: 12

FATS PER SERVING: FAT FREE

Notes: _____

_____

_____

_____

Rating For This Recipe
❏ Poor ❏ Fair
❏ Good ❏ Excellent

SUNDAY SALAD

1 large box SUGAR FREE apricot gelatin (or any flavor)
2 cups boiling water
2 cups cold water
1 cup crushed pineapple (drained) save juice
2 bananas sliced
1 cup marshmallows

METHOD:
Mix gelatin with water.
Add pineapple, marshmallows, bananas
and let stand until firm.

Topping:
1/2 cup sugar
4 ounces egg substitute
1/2 cup pineapple juice
2 tablespoons flour
2 tablespoons famous brand FAT FREE margarine
1 large package FAT FREE cream cheese
1 package dry whipped topping prepared with skim milk.
Cook sugar, egg, pineapple juice, flour and margarine until
it begins to thicken.
Add cream cheese, then dry whipped topping.
Spread over gelatin.

SERVES: 6-8

FATS PER SERVING: TRACE

Rating For This Recipe	Notes: _____
❏ Poor ❏ Fair	_____
❏ Good ❏ Excellent	_____

LAYERED SALAD #1

1/2 head lettuce, shredded
1/2 cup diced celery
3 hard-boiled eggs, sliced, WHITES ONLY
1/2 package frozen peas, uncooked
1/4 chopped onion
4 slices turkey bacon (cooked crisp and crumbled)
1 cup FAT FREE Miracle Whip salad dressing
1 tablespoon sugar
2 ounces FAT FREE shredded Cheddar cheese

METHOD:
Put in 9 X 13-inch dish first 6 ingredients in order given
in recipe.
Mix Miracle Whip salad dressing and sugar for salad.
DO NOT MIX SALAD
Top with shredded Cheddar cheese.
Refrigerate 8 to 24 hours.
You can mix lightly before serving or serve as is without
mixing, whichever you prefer.

SERVES: 8

FATS PER SERVING: 1

Notes: _____

_____

_____

_____

Rating For This Recipe	
❏ Poor	❏ Fair
❏ Good	❏ Excellent

LAYERED SALAD #2

1 head of lettuce, torn into bite-size pieces
1 cup diced green pepper
1/4 cup sliced green onions
1 10-ounce package frozen peas, uncooked
2 cups FAT FREE Miracle Whip
2 cups FAT FREE Cheddar cheese

METHOD :
In a 13 x 9 x 2-inch pan, layer
lettuce, green peppers, onions and peas.
DO NOT TOSS.
Spread salad dressing over all.
Sprinkle with cheese. Cover and refrigerate overnight.

SERVES: 8-10

FATS PER SERVING: FAT FREE

Notes: _____

Rating For This Recipe
❑ Poor ❑ Fair
❑ Good ❑ Excellent

_____

_____

_____

MOM'S POTATO SALAD

8 cups cooked and quartered potatoes
1 cup diced onion
3 tablespoons celery seed
1 cup dill pickles
3 teaspoons salt
1 teaspoon pepper
1 tablespoon prepared mustard
3 hard cooked egg whites (discard yolks)
1 cup FAT FREE Miracle Whip salad dressing

METHOD:
Mix above ingredients in a large
bowl until well-blended.
Chill.

Serves 8-10

FATS PER SERVING: FAT FREE

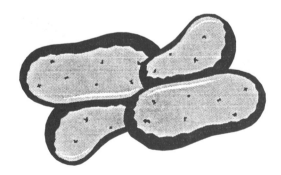

Notes: _____

_____

_____

_____

Rating For This Recipe	
❑ Poor	❑ Fair
❑ Good	❑ Excellent

ORANGE CHEESE SALAD

1 small carton FAT FREE cottage cheese (small curd)
1 can mandarin oranges, cut up
1 small package SUGAR FREE orange gelatin (dry)
6 ounces dry whipped topping mix prepared with skim milk

METHOD:
Mix cottage cheese and dry gelatin.
Add whipped topping and drained orange pieces.
Let set.
Serve on lettuce leaves.
Can also be made with drained, crushed pineapple and
other flavors of gelatin.

SERVES: 4-6

FATS PER SERVING: FAT FREE

Rating For This Recipe	Notes: _____
❑ Poor ❑ Fair	_____
❑ Good ❑ Excellent	_____

PINE/BERRY SALAD

1 small package SUGAR FREE strawberry gelatin
1/2 cup hot water
1 medium can cranberry sauce (use whole cranberry sauce)
1 small can crushed pineapple, drained

METHOD:
Dissolve gelatin in hot water.
Mix in cranberry sauce and pineapple.
When firm, add topping.

Topping:
1 3-ounce package FAT FREE cream cheese
1/2 pint container dry whipped topping
prepared with skim milk
1/4 cup sugar
Mix together and spread on top of above mixture.

SERVES: 4-6

FATS PER SERVING: FAT FREE

Notes: _____

_____

_____

_____

Rating For This Recipe
❑ Poor   ❑ Fair
❑ Good   ❑ Excellent

PINEAPPLE MOLD

1 package SUGAR FREE lime or strawberry gelatin (small box)
1 cup hot water
1 cup canned pineapple juice
1/8 teaspoon salt
1 egg white

METHOD:
Dissolve gelatin in hot water.
Add the pineapple juice and salt.
Chill until slightly thickened.
Place in a bowl of ice water.
Add the egg white and whip with electric mixer until
fluffy and thick.
Pile lightly into sherbet glasses.
Chill until firm.

SERVES: 6

FATS PER SERVING: FAT FREE

Rating For This Recipe
❏ Poor ❏ Fair
❏ Good ❏ Excellent

Notes: _____

_____

_____

_____

PINEAPPLE ORANGE SALAD

1 large package (6 ounce) SUGAR FREE orange gelatin
2 1/2 cups boiling water
6-ounce can frozen orange juice, undiluted
1 20-ounce can crushed pineapple, undrained
(Use pineapple in its own juice)
1 16-ounce can mandarin oranges, drained
1 3-ounce box SUGAR FREE instant lemon pudding
prepared with skim milk
1 package dry whipped topping

METHOD:
In a large bowl, dissolve the gelatin in boiling water.
Add pineapple and juice, orange juice and mandarin oranges.
Stir until juice is thawed.
Pour into a 9 x 13 pan and allow to set in refrigerator.
Meanwhile, mix lemon pudding with
1 cup of skim milk and set aside.
Prepare whipped topping according to package directions
using skim milk.
By this time, the pudding will be set.
Fold it into the whipped topping and spread it
over the gelatin mixture.
Chill.
This is very good for preparing ahead of time, covering
well with plastic wrap until ready to serve.

SERVES: 9

FATS PER SERVING: TRACE

Notes: _____

_____

_____

_____

Rating For This Recipe
❏ Poor ❏ Fair
❏ Good ❏ Excellent

PISTACHIO SALAD

1 16-ounce can crushed pineapple
1 package dry whipped topping prepared with skim milk
1 small box SUGAR FREE pistachio pudding mix
2 cups small marshmallows

METHOD:
Mix pineapple and pudding mix.
Let sit 5 minutes.
Add remaining ingredients and mix together and let set.

SERVES: 4-6

FATS PER SERVING: FAT FREE

"Feel tied up?
Join LFC!"

Rating For This Recipe
❏ Poor ❏ Fair
❏ Good ❏ Excellent

Notes: _____
_____
_____
_____

PRETZEL SALAD

1st Layer:
1 cup crushed FAT FREE pretzels
1/4 cup sugar
4 tablespoons slightly melted FAT FREE margarine
Mix together and put in the bottom of
9 x 13 pan. Put in freezer
2nd layer:
8 ounces dry whipped topping prepared with skim milk
1 8-ounce FAT FREE cream cheese, softened
1/4 cup sugar
Mix together and place on top of 1st layer. Chill.
3rd layer:
1 can crushed pineapple, drained, reserve juice
1/4 cup sugar
2 tablespoons cornstarch

METHOD:
Drain 1 1/2 cups juice from pineapple (add water if necessary)
Mix small amount of juice with cornstarch and sugar that
have been mixed together and stir.
Continue to add juice slowly.
Cook over medium heat until thickened.
Add pineapple and cool .
Spread on top of 2nd layer. Chill.
May serve as salad or dessert.
SERVES: 8-10

FATS PER SERVING: TRACE
WATCH THOSE CALORIES!

Notes: _____

_____

_____

_____

Rating For This Recipe
❏ Poor ❏ Fair
❏ Good ❏ Excellent

SAWDUST SALAD

1 3-ounce package SUGAR FREE lemon gelatin
1 3-ounce package SUGAR FREE orange gelatin
2 cups boiling water
1 1/2 cups cold water
2 bananas, diced
1 can crushed pineapple (drained and juice reserved)
40 miniature marshmallows

METHOD:
Dissolve gelatins in boiling water.
Stir in the cold water and add fruit and marshmallows.
Chill until set.
Top with the following:
1/2 cup sugar
2 tablespoons flour
1 cup reserved pineapple juice (add water if necessary)
1/4 cup egg substitute (equals 1 egg)

METHOD:
In a saucepan, stir flour and sugar together and slowly
add juice and egg substitute.
Cook over medium heat until thick, stirring constantly.
Spread over the gelatin mixture after cooked mixture has cooled.
Mix: 1 FAT FREE package cream cheese and 2 cups dry whipped
topping prepared with skim milk and spread over cooked mixture.
Sprinkle with FAT FREE grated Cheddar cheese
evenly over the top.

SERVES: 12

FATS PER SERVING: TRACE

Rating For This Recipe
☐ Poor ☐ Fair
☐ Good ☐ Excellent

Notes: _____
_____
_____
_____

STRAWBERRY SALAD

2 packages SUGAR FREE strawberry gelatin
1 1/2 cups boiling water
2 packages frozen strawberries
1 medium can crushed pineapple (drained)
2 bananas mashed

METHOD:
Dissolve gelatin in boiling water.
Add frozen strawberries immediately.
Chill until partially set.
Fold in pineapple and bananas.
Put half of mixture in 9 x 12 pan.
Whip 2 envelopes of dry whipped topping prepared
with skim milk and 8-ounce package of FAT FREE
cream cheese.
Spread on first layer of jelled gelatin, then spread rest of
remaining gelatin on top and chill.

SERVES: 6-8

FATS PER SERVING: FAT FREE

Notes: _____
_____
_____
_____

Rating For This Recipe	
❏ Poor	❏ Fair
❏ Good	❏ Excellent

SUNNY SALAD

1 8-ounce can crushed pineapple in its own juice, drained
1 pound peeled and shredded carrots
1 16-ounce carton FAT FREE sour cream
1 cup raisins
Sweeten to taste
1/2 teaspoon almond extract (may substitute vanilla,
orange or coconut extract if desired)

METHOD:
Mix ingredients and chill several hours
to allow flavors to blend.

SERVES: 6-8

FATS PER SERVING: FAT FREE

"Soar to new heights with LFC."

Rating For This Recipe	Notes: _____
☐ Poor   ☐ Fair
☐ Good   ☐ Excellent

SUNSET SALAD

1 6-ounce package SUGAR FREE orange gelatin
1/2 teaspoon salt
1 2/3 cups boiling water
1 cup crushed pineapple in juice
1 tablespoon lemon juice OR vinegar
1 cup grated carrots

METHOD:
Dissolve gelatin and salt in boiling water.
Add pineapple and juice.
Add carrots and lemon juice (or vinegar).
Chill 2 hours.

SERVES: 6

FATS PER SERVING: FAT FREE

Notes: _____

_____

_____

_____

Rating For This Recipe
❑ Poor ❑ Fair
❑ Good ❑ Excellent

A GOOD PARENT

Take one gentle smiling face
Add 1 full measure of understanding
A few tender touches with 2 loving hands,
1 lifelong mind full of love and forgiveness
A soft voice with firmness added as needed
2 lips to say a prayer each day
— — — For Health, Happiness and Guidance
1 strong desire for cleanliness of
— — — Home, Soul, Mind and Body.
Add this to: One body with 2 feet willing to run errands;
But can stand firm in their belief of
— — — Obedience, Kindness and Respect
For "God" and all mankind.
2 eyes that close each night knowing that
each ingredient has done its best
Thro' the Day, and All Is Well Don

— Unknown —

"There sure are a lot of good ingredients in this recipe!"

RATE YOURSELF!

Rating For This Recipe
❏ Poor ❏ Fair
❏ Good ❏ Excellent

Notes: _____
_____
_____
_____

WAX BEAN SALAD

1 can wax beans drained
1 small onion chopped
Dash of parsley flakes
2 teaspoons chopped pimento
1 package sweetener
2 tablespoons FAT FREE Miracle Whip

METHOD:
Mix all ingredients in a bowl and chill.

SERVES: 4

FATS PER SERVING: FAT FREE

"I can find everything I need at the grocery."

Notes: _____

_____

_____

_____

Rating For This Recipe
❏ Poor ❏ Fair
❏ Good ❏ Excellent

VEGGIES:

BAKED MACARONI AND CHEESE

2 cups macaroni
1/2 pound FAT FREE grated cheese
4 tablespoons famous brand FAT FREE margarine
2 tablespoons flour
1/4 teaspoon salt
2 cups skim milk

METHOD:
Cook macaroni in boiling, salted water until tender.
While macaroni is cooking, melt margarine in pan.
Blend in flour, salt and milk.
Add 3/4 of cheese and stir to melt.
Put macaroni in a sprayed 2-quart casserole dish and pour sauce over, stirring to coat macaroni.
Sprinkle remaining cheese over top.
Bake at 325 degrees for 20 to 30 minutes.

SERVES: 6

FATS PER SERVING: TRACE

Rating For This Recipe
❑ Poor ❑ Fair
❑ Good ❑ Excellent

Notes: _____
_____
_____
_____

BAKED RICE DISH

1 1/2 cups white cooked rice
Sauté until tender, 1 medium onion
1 pound ground turkey breast (cooked)

METHOD:
Add:
8 ounces mushroom soup
1 can mushrooms
1 cup grated (fine) carrots
1/2 cup Half &Half cream
1 cup grated FAT FREE Cheddar cheese
1 4-ounce carton egg substitute
Lite cooking spray
Bake 50 minutes in greased baking dish at 350 degrees.
Freezes well before baking.

SERVES: 6

FATS PER SERVING: 3

Notes: _____

_____

_____

_____

Rating For This Recipe	
❑ Poor	❑ Fair
❑ Good	❑ Excellent

SCALLOPED ASPARAGUS

Preheat oven to 325 degrees

4 cups fresh asparagus cut into 1-inch pieces
1 1/2 cups skim milk
2 tablespoons flour
1 teaspoon salt
1/2 teaspoon pepper
1/2 cup grated FAT FREE American cheese
1 cup FAT FREE bread crumbs
2 tablespoons FAT FREE margarine

METHOD:
Cook asparagus pieces in a small amount of water
until crisp and tender.
Transfer to a baking dish that has been sprayed with
non-stick butter-flavored cooking spray.
Combine in a small bowl the milk, flour, salt and pepper
and add to the asparagus.
Add half of the FAT FREE cheese and bread crumbs and
and stir through gently.
Add remaining cheese and crumbs to top of mixture and
dot with FAT FREE margarine.
Bake 30 minutes or until brown on top.

SERVES: 4-6

FATS PER SERVING: FAT FREE

Rating For This Recipe
❑ Poor ❑ Fair
❑ Good ❑ Excellent

Notes: _____
_____
_____
_____

BROCCOLI & CAULIFLOWER ITALIANO

1 head cauliflower broken into flowerets
1 bunch fresh broccoli cut into flowerets
1 green bell pepper cut into strips

METHOD:
Mix vegetables well and pour your
favorite FAT FREE Italian dressing over all.
Marinate several hours, tossing often to
moisten.

SERVES: 4

FATS PER SERVING: FAT FREE

"I like
to eat!"

Notes: _____

_____

_____

_____

Rating For This Recipe
❏ Poor ❏ Fair
❏ Good ❏ Excellent

BAKED CREAMED POTATOES

Preheat oven to 375 degrees.
1/2 cup skim milk
2 tablespoons famous brand FAT FREE margarine
2 tablespoons flour
I teaspoon salt
1/4 teaspoon black pepper
1/2 teaspoon celery salt
1/4 cup chopped parsley OR
1/2 tablespoon dried parsley flakes
3 cups diced cooked potatoes
(4 or 5 medium potatoes)
1 cup FAT FREE bread crumbs
2 tablespoons famous brand FAT FREE margarine, melted

METHOD:

Spray 1 1/2-quart casserole with non-stick cooking spray
Make a soup in a large saucepan by melting 2 tablespoons
of the FAT FREE margarine and stirring in the flour, salt,
pepper and skim milk. Let it bubble up.
Remove from heat and slowly stir to blend.
Return to heat and stir until thickened and smooth.
Remove from heat and stir in the celery salt, parsley and
the potatoes. Pour into the prepared casserole.
Combine the bread crumbs and the melted margarine,
sprinkle evenly over top of the casserole.
Bake for about 20 minutes or until hot and well-browned.

SERVES: 4

FATS PER SERVING: TRACE

Rating For This Recipe
❑ Poor ❑ Fair
❑ Good ❑ Excellent

Notes: _____

_____

_____

_____

BAKED LIMA BEANS IN TOMATO SAUCE

1 package dried lima beans cooked and
drained, reserving 1/2 cup liquid
2 8-ounce cans tomato sauce
1 cup chopped onion
1/4 cup light brown sugar, firmly packed
2 teaspoons prepared mustard
2 teaspoons Worcestershire sauce
1/2 teaspoon oregano

METHOD:
In medium saucepan spray with butter-flavored
cooking spray.
Sauté onions over low heat until tender.
Combine other ingredients, including reserved liquid
and mix until well-blended.
Turn into a 2-quart shallow baking dish that has been
sprayed with cooking spray.
Bake at 350 degrees for 45 minutes.

SERVES: 6

FATS PER SERVING: TRACE

Notes: _____

_____

_____

_____

Rating For This Recipe
❑ Poor ❑ Fair
❑ Good ❑ Excellent

BREADED TOMATOES

3 large ripe tomatoes peeled and cut
into pieces OR one can of tomatoes
1 teaspoon salt
1 teaspoon sweet basil
1 medium onion (chopped)
1/2 teaspoon pepper
1 small green pepper (chopped)

METHOD:
Mix tomatoes, onion, green
pepper, salt and pepper in saucepan.
Cover and heat to boiling.
Reduce heat and simmer until green pepper and onion
are tender, 8-10 minutes.
Stir in 4 slices of FAT FREE bread that has been torn in
small pieces and 1 package of sweetener.

SERVES: 4

FATS PER SERVING: FAT FREE

Rating For This Recipe
❑ Poor ❑ Fair
❑ Good ❑ Excellent

Notes: _____
_____
_____
_____

CABBAGE AU GRATIN

1 1/2 pounds of cabbage cut in thin wedges
and cooked until tender in a
small amount of water.

MAKE A WHITE SAUCE USING:
2 tablespoons FAT FREE margarine
5 tablespoons flour
1 3/4 cups skim milk
2 cups shredded FAT FREE American cheese

METHOD:
Alternate layers of cabbage and white sauce in a
sprayed 9 X 13 baking dish, ending with white sauce.
Sprinkle cheese evenly over top.
Bake in a 350-degree oven for 20 minutes.

SERVES: 4

FATS PER SERVING: TRACE

Notes: _____

_____

_____

_____

CARROTS & PEA PODS in ORANGE SAUCE

1 cup sliced carrots
2 cups FRESH pea pods OR
1 6-ounce package frozen pea pods
1/3 cup orange juice
1 teaspoon cornstarch
2 teaspoons low sodium soy sauce
1 teaspoon finely shredded orange peel

METHOD:
Cook carrots in small amount of boiling salted
water in a covered medium-sized saucepan for 5 minutes.
Add pea pods and cook 2 to 4 minutes more or until
vegetables are crisp-tender.   DRAIN.
Return vegetables to saucepan and cover to keep warm.

Orange Sauce:
In small saucepan, combine orange juice and cornstarch
until well-blended.
Cook and stir over medium heat until mixture is thickened
and then stir in orange peel and soy sauce.
Pour over vegetables and toss to cover.

SERVES: 4

FATS PER SERVING: FAT FREE

Rating For This Recipe
❏ Poor ❏ Fair
❏ Good ❏ Excellent

Notes: _____
_____
_____
_____

CHEESY POTATOES

4 medium potatoes, washed, pared and cut into thin rounds
1 cup FAT FREE shredded sharp Cheddar cheese
1 medium onion sliced and made into rings
3 tablespoons flour
1 1/2 tablespoons famous brand FAT FREE margarine
1 1/2 cups skim milk
Salt and pepper to taste

METHOD:
Mix potatoes, onion, flour, salt and pepper.
Pour in a sprayed 9 x 13 baking dish.
Spread FAT FREE cheese over top.
Pour skim milk over all.
Dot with 1 1/2 tablespoons FAT FREE margarine.
Bake for 35 minutes in a 350-degree oven.

SERVES: 4

FATS PER SERVING: TRACE

Notes: _____

_____

_____

_____

Rating For This Recipe
❏ Poor ❏ Fair
❏ Good ❏ Excellent

CORN SOUFFLÉ

2 cups cream-style corn (NOTE: Make sure nutritional label reads TOTAL FAT 0)
6 teaspoons flour
1 carton egg substitute (equals 4 eggs)
2 cups skim milk
4 slices FAT FREE bread
1 tablespoon FAT FREE famous brand margarine
4 slices FAT FREE bread made into crumbs

METHOD:
Combine first 5 ingredients
and mix lightly.
Put in a casserole dish that has been sprayed with butter-flavored cooking spray.
Top with the bread crumbs.
Bake for 30 minutes at 350 degrees or until bubbly.

SERVES: 4

FATS PER SERVING: TRACE

Rating For This Recipe
❏ Poor ❏ Fair
❏ Good ❏ Excellent

Notes: _____
_____
_____
_____

CORN PUDDING

3 tablespoons FAT FREE famous brand margarine
1 box famous name corn bread mix
1 carton egg substitute (8 ounces)
1 can cream-style corn (NOTE: Make sure nutritional label reads TOTAL FAT 0)
1 can whole kernel corn (do not drain)
8 ounces FAT FREE sour cream

METHOD:
Melt the margarine in a 2-quart glass dish in the microwave for a couple of seconds.
In a large bowl, mix the rest of the ingredients and pour in a two-quart casserole dish.
Diced onions may be placed on top if desired.
Bake for 1 hour in a 350-degree oven uncovered.

SERVES: 4

FATS PER SERVING: 1

Notes: _____
_____
_____
_____

Rating For This Recipe
❏ Poor   ❏ Fair
❏ Good   ❏ Excellent

CORN PUDDING II

1/2 cup egg substitute (equals 2 eggs)
1 tablespoon sugar
2 tablespoons all-purpose flour
1 teaspoon salt
1 cup skim milk
1 can cream-style corn (NOTE: Make sure nutritional label reads TOTAL FAT 0)

METHOD:
Spray 2-quart casserole with butter-flavored cooking spray.
Mix ingredients well and pour into prepared dish.
Bake for 1 hour at 350 degrees.

SERVES: 4-6

FATS PER SERVING: FAT FREE

Rating For This Recipe
❑ Poor ❑ Fair
❑ Good ❑ Excellent

Notes: _____
_____
_____
_____

DOWN-HOME BEANS AND ONIONS

1 can of your favorite beans (pinto, navy, great northern, lima or kidney)
2 tablespoons dried onion soup mix

METHOD:
Mix ingredients in a small saucepan and bring to a boil on medium high heat.
Lower heat to simmer.
Cover pan and allow to simmer 20-25 minutes.

SERVINGS: 2-4

FATS PER SERVING: FAT FREE

Notes: _____

_____

_____

_____

Rating For This Recipe	
❑ Poor	❑ Fair
❑ Good	❑ Excellent

DOWN HOME BLACK EYED PEAS

2 cans black-eyed peas
1 medium onion (chopped)
1/2 teaspoon salt
1/4 teaspoon black pepper
1 chicken bouillon cube

METHOD:
Place beans, juice and all, onion, salt, pepper
and bouillon cube in saucepan.
Cover.
Bring to a boil, then reduce heat to simmer.
Simmer for 1 1/2 hours, stirring occasionally.

SERVES: 6-8

FATS PER SERVING: FAT FREE

"Just cut through the
paperwork and get to
the bottomline...
LFC can do the job!"

Rating For This Recipe
❏ Poor ❏ Fair
❏ Good ❏ Excellent

Notes: _____
_____
_____
_____

EASY BAKED BEANS

2 1-pound cans pork and beans in tomato sauce
1 small can crushed pineapple, drained
1 small onion, chopped
1 teaspoon dry mustard
2 tablespoons brown sugar substitute
1/2 cup catsup
3 slices TURKEY bacon

METHOD:
Mix beans, pineapple, onion, mustard, brown sugar and catsup.
Pour into casserole.
Add cut-up bacon on top.
Bake in 350-degree oven for about 1 1/2 hours.

SERVES: 8

FATS PER SERVING: 2

Notes: _____

_____

_____

_____

Rating For This Recipe
❑ Poor ❑ Fair
❑ Good ❑ Excellent

FAT-FREE FRIED POTATOES:

Prepare potatoes as normal to fry slice as thin as possible.

METHOD:
Spray Teflon skillet with a non-sticking cooking spray.
Add potatoes.
Salt and pepper to taste.
Cook on low heat till done.
In the last few minutes, you can turn heat up to brown.

FATS PER SERVING: FAT FREE

Rating For This Recipe	Notes: _____
❑ Poor ❑ Fair	_____
❑ Good ❑ Excellent	_____

"FRIED" HASH BROWNS

potatoes
1 small onion (optional)

METHOD:
Wash, peel and soak in cold water
and refrigerate for several hours one or more
large potatoes (allow 1 per serving).
When ready to cook, drain and pat potato dry and grate.
May grate small onion at this time and add to potato if desired.
Preheat skillet and remove from stove.
Aiming away from burner, spray with butter-flavored
cooking spray and add potato and/or onion if desired.
Cover and cook on medium heat until bottom is brown.
Remove skillet from heat and away from stove, spray top of
potatoes with butter-flavored cooking spray and turn over,
pressing and flattening potatoes.
Continue cooking until potatoes are done and bottom is
nicely browned.

SERVES: ONE OR MORE

FATS PER SERVING: FAT FREE

Notes: _____

_____

_____

_____

Rating For This Recipe
❏ Poor ❏ Fair
❏ Good ❏ Excellent

GOLDEN CARROTS SUPREME

3/4 cup FAT FREE chicken broth OR bouillon
2 teaspoons salt
Pepper to taste
2 teaspoons sugar
5 cups cleaned carrots that have been
diagonally sliced 1/4-inch thick
2 teaspoons lemon juice (may use reconstituted)
1/4 chopped fresh parsley OR 1 1/2 tablespoons dried
parsley flakes

METHOD:
Bring broth or bouillon to a boil.
Stir in salt, pepper, sugar and carrots.
Simmer, covered until carrots are crisp tender.
Stir in lemon juice and parsley.

SERVES: 6

FATS PER SERVING: FAT FREE

Notes: _____

_____

_____

_____

GLAZED JULIENNE CARROTS

1 pound carrots cut in julienne strips
1/4 cup water
2 tablespoons FAT FREE famous brand margarine
3 tablespoons sugar
Nutmeg OR chopped mint

METHOD:
In a saucepan, place carrots in water, cover and
cook over low heat (about 10 minutes)
until carrots are crisp tender.
Remove lid, add FAT FREE margarine and sugar and
continue cooking until carrots are tender and well-glazed.
Stir frequently.
When done, sprinkle with nutmeg or mint.

SERVES: 6

FATS PER SERVING: FAT FREE

Notes: _____
_____
_____
_____

Rating For This Recipe	
❏ Poor	❏ Fair
❏ Good	❏ Excellent

GREEN BEAN MARINADE

1 can French-style green beans drained
1/4 cup coarsely chopped onion
1 small can mushroom slices
1/2 head cauliflowerets (optional)

Toss the above ingredients together and set aside.
In a small bowl, mix thoroughly:
1/4 cup red wine vinegar
1/4 cup water
1 clove finely minced garlic OR
1/4 teaspoon garlic powder
3 packs sweetener (or to taste)

METHOD:
Pour above mixture over the vegetables and mix well.
Refrigerate overnight.
Mix well before serving.

SERVES: 4

FATS PER SERVING: FAT FREE

Rating For This Recipe
❏ Poor ❏ Fair
❏ Good ❏ Excellent

Notes: _____
_____
_____
_____

GREEN PEAS AND MUSHROOMS

2 1/2 cups fresh peas
1 cup sliced fresh mushrooms
2 tablespoons chopped onion
1 tablespoon FAT FREE famous brand margarine

METHOD:
Cook peas in small amount of water in a small
saucepan until tender.
Spray large skillet with butter-flavored cooking spray and
sauté mushrooms and onions until tender.
Drain peas of remaining water.
Add peas and FAT FREE margarine to other vegetables.
Mix well to coat vegetables with margarine.

SERVES: 4-6

FATS PER SERVING: FAT FREE

Notes: _____

_____

_____ | **Rating For This Recipe**
_____   ❑ Poor ❑ Fair
❑ Good ❑ Excellent

HOMINY

1 can hominy (#2 size)
1 chicken bouillon cube
2 teaspoons salt
1/4 teaspoon black pepper

METHOD:
Place above ingredients in saucepan, cover and
bring to a boil.
Reduce heat and cook until liquid is reduced by half.
Uncover and reduce liquid by half again.

SERVES: 4

FATS PER SERVING: FAT FREE

Rating For This Recipe
❏ Poor ❏ Fair
❏ Good ❏ Excellent

Notes: _____
_____
_____
_____

MEXICAN CORN

Heat skillet. Removing from burner,
spray skillet with non-stick cooking spray,
aiming away from burner.
Place in skillet:
1 10-ounce package frozen whole yellow corn
1/2 cup chopped green pepper
1 crushed clove of garlic
2 tablespoons FAT FREE famous brand margarine
1 tablespoon of pimiento
Salt and pepper to taste

METHOD:
Cover and simmer vegetables
for 10 minutes, stirring often to keep from sticking.
Stir in pimiento pieces (1 tablespoon) and
continue cooking until corn is tender.
If necessary, use a little warm water to prevent sticking.
When corn is tender, remove from heat and stir in
2 tablespoons FAT FREE margarine.
Serve immediately.

SERVES: 4

FATS PER SERVING: FAT FREE

Notes: _____

_____

_____

_____

Rating For This Recipe
❑ Poor ❑ Fair
❑ Good ❑ Excellent

MEXICALI CORN

1 can cream-style corn (NOTE: Make sure nutritional
label reads TOTAL FAT 0)
1 can whole kernel corn, drained
1/4 cup green bell pepper
2 tablespoons pimiento, minced
Dash of tobasco
1 teaspoon salt
1/2 teaspoon pepper
1/2 cup FAT FREE bread crumbs

METHOD:
Mix all ingredients but bread crumbs
and place in a butter-flavored sprayed
2-quart casserole dish.
Top with bread crumbs.
Spray crumbs with butter-flavored spray.
Bake 30 minutes at 350 degrees

SERVES: 4-6

FATS PER SERVING: TRACE

Rating For This Recipe	Notes: _____
❑ Poor ❑ Fair	_____
❑ Good ❑ Excellent	_____

OVEN "FRENCH FRIED" POTATOES

Preheat oven to 400 degrees

Scrub 1 large baking potato per serving
Cut potatoes (with skin on) as for French fries.
1 or 2 slightly beaten egg whites
(depends on number of potatoes used.)
Seasoned salt to your liking: (Cajun, celery, etc.)

METHOD:
Dip potato sticks in egg white
and place on cookie sheet that has been sprayed
with cooking spray.
Sprinkle with seasoned salt.
Bake 20-30 minutes, stirring sticks often.
Bake until crispy and brown.

FATS PER SERVING: FAT FREE

Notes: _____

_____

_____

_____

Rating For This Recipe	
❑ Poor	❑ Fair
❑ Good	❑ Excellent

PAN "FRIED" EGGPLANT

1 medium-size eggplant peeled
and sliced 3/4 inches thick
3/4 cup Italian seasoned FAT FREE bread crumbs
1 egg white, slightly beaten

METHOD:
Dip each slice of eggplant
into the slightly beaten egg white.
Dip in seasoned bread crumbs and coat on both sides.
Preheat skillet and remove from stove.
Facing away from heat source, spray skillet with
butter-flavored cooking spray.
Return skillet to heat.
Add eggplant and fry over low heat until browned.
Turn once to brown other side.
May serve plain or covered in tomato sauce.

SERVES: 2-4

FATS PER SERVING: FAT FREE

Notes: _____

Rating For This Recipe
❏ Poor ❏ Fair
❏ Good ❏ Excellent

_____

_____

_____

PEAS AND DUMPLINGS

1 16-ounce package frozen peas, cooked according to
package directions
1/4 cup egg substitute (equals 1 egg)
1/3 cup skim evaporated milk
Flour to form soft dough
Boiling water in a saucepan

METHOD:
Mix egg substitute in milk and flour.
Take a small amount of dough on tip of knife and drop
in the boiling water. Dumpling will slide off.
Continue with remaining dough.
Cook 3-5 minutes.
Mix with peas.
Stir in FAT FREE famous brand margarine.

SERVES: 4-6

FATS PER SERVING: FAT FREE

Notes: _____

_____

_____

_____

Rating For This Recipe	
❑ Poor	❑ Fair
❑ Good	❑ Excellent

POLYNESIAN PEA PODS

8 ounces fresh sugar pea pods
1 can (8 1/4 ounces) pineapple chunks, drained
2 tablespoons FAT FREE famous brand margarine
1/4 teaspoon salt

METHOD:
Wash pea pods and remove tips and strings.
Heat 1 inch of salted water in a sauce pan to boiling.
Add pods. Heat to boiling and cook uncovered, stirring
occasionally, until crisp tender, 2-3 minutes.
Drain.
Put back in pan and cover to keep warm.
Spray skillet with butter-flavored cooking spray
and add drained pineapple chunks.
Heat over low heat until hot, gently stirring occasionally.
When heated through, add pea pods, FAT FREE margarine
and toss to coat and heat through.

SERVES: 4

FATS PER SERVING: FAT FREE

Rating For This Recipe	
☐ Poor	☐ Fair
☐ Good	☐ Excellent

Notes: _____
_____
_____
_____

"RECYCLED" POTATO PANCAKES

2 cups left-over mashed potatoes
1/2 cup finely minced onion
1/4 cup egg substitute
1/4 cup all-purpose flour
1 teaspoon baking powder

METHOD:
Prepare skillet by preheating.
Then facing away from stove, spray with
non-stick cooking spray.
Mix above ingredients thoroughly.
Drop mixture by large tablespoon onto the hot skillet.
Brown first on one side, then the other over a medium
low heat.
Keep warm in a slow oven until batter is used up.

SERVES: 4

FATS PER SERVING: TRACE

Notes: _____

_____

_____

_____

Rating For This Recipe
❑ Poor ❑ Fair
❑ Good ❑ Excellent

SAVORY MASHED POTATOES

12 medium potatoes, peeled
1 8-ounce package FAT FREE cream cheese
1 cup FAT FREE sour cream
1 tablespoon chopped chives
2 teaspoons salt
1/8 teaspoon pepper
1 clove garlic, crushed OR 1/2 teaspoon garlic powder
1/4 teaspoon paprika

METHOD:
Cook potatoes in boiling salted water until tender.
Drain.
In a large bowl, mash potatoes with an electric mixer.
Add cream cheese and sour cream, pepper and garlic.
Beat on high speed until smooth and light.
Stir in chives.
Spoon into a baking dish that has been sprayed with
butter-flavored cooking spray.
Sprinkle with paprika.
Bake 30 minutes in a 350-degree oven or until golden
brown and heated through.
This can also be prepared ahead of time and frozen
before baking.

SERVES: 6-8

FATS PER SERVING: FAT FREE

Rating For This Recipe
❑ Poor ❑ Fair
❑ Good ❑ Excellent

Notes: _____
_____
_____
_____

SCALLOPED CORN

2 tablespoons famous brand FAT FREE margarine
2 tablespoons flour
1 cup skim milk
1 teaspoon salt
1 cup buttered FAT FREE bread crumbs
2 teaspoons sugar
1/8 teaspoon pepper
1 12-ounce can whole kernel corn (1 1/2 cups)
(NOTE: Make sure nutritional label reads TOTAL FAT 0)
1/2 cup grated FAT FREE cheese

METHOD:
Melt margarine and blend in flour until smooth.
Add milk gradually, stirring constantly.
Add salt, sugar, pepper and corn.
Cover bottom of sprayed baking dish with a layer of corn
and sprinkle with buttered crumbs and grated cheese.
Bake until brown about 20 to 30 minutes.
Brown the crumbs in 1/4 cup margarine melted in
heavy-bottomed skillet.

Serves: 4

FATS PER SERVING: TRACE

Notes: _____

_____

_____

_____

Rating For This Recipe
❑ Poor   ❑ Fair
❑ Good   ❑ Excellent

SCALLOPED POTATOES

8 or 9 potatoes
1 cup FAT FREE cheese
1 1/2 cups skim milk
4 tablespoons FAT FREE famous brand margarine
Onions
Salt and pepper to taste
Flour

METHOD:
Slice potatoes (not too thin).
Shake in a paper sack with flour, salt and pepper.
Add 1 cup FAT FREE cheese and some minced onions.
Spray a baking dish and add all ingredients.
Add 1 1/2 cups skim milk and 4 tablespoons
FAT FREE margarine.
Bake about 1 hour.

SERVES: 8-9

FATS PER SERVING: FAT FREE

Rating For This Recipe
❑ Poor ❑ Fair
❑ Good ❑ Excellent

Notes: _____
_____
_____
_____

SOUPER GREEN BEANS

2 cans French-style green beans
2 teaspoons dry onion soup mix with mushrooms

METHOD:
Drain liquid from one can of the green beans.
Place beans and 2nd can of beans in sauce pan.
Stir in dry soup mix.
Stir well to mix and bring to a boil.
Reduce heat, cover and simmer for 45 minutes to an hour

SERVES: 6-8

FATS PER SERVING: FAT FREE

Don't panic!
LFC can help!

Notes: _____

_____

_____

_____

Rating For This Recipe
❏ Poor ❏ Fair
❏ Good ❏ Excellent

STEAMED HERBED VEGETABLES

1 cup broccoli flowerets
1 cup cauliflower flowerets
1/2 cup pieces sweet red pepper cut in 1-inch slices
1/2 cup sliced fresh mushrooms
1 tablespoon fresh marjoram OR 1/8 teaspoon dried
1/4 teaspoon dried oregano
1/8 teaspoon dried rosemary
1/4 teaspoon salt
1/8 teaspoon pepper
1 tablespoon water
1 tablespoon FAT FREE famous brand margarine

METHOD:
Combine all ingredients in a 1 1/2-quart
microwave-safe casserole.
Cover tightly with plastic wrap, folding back a small edge
to allow steam to escape.
Microwave on HIGH 3 1/2 minutes or until crisp-tender,
stirring once.

SERVES: 4

FATS PER SERVING: FAT FREE

Rating For This Recipe
❏ Poor ❏ Fair
❏ Good ❏ Excellent

Notes: _____
_____
_____
_____

SUNDAY DINNER POTATOES

1 cup FAT FREE sour cream
2 cups NO FAT cottage cheese
2 teaspoons salt
2 tablespoons minced onion
1 clove garlic, minced
6 medium-sized potatoes, peeled, cooked and diced
1/2 cup shredded FAT FREE Cheddar cheese
Paprika

METHOD:
Spray 1 1/2-quart casserole with non-stick cooking spray.
In a bowl, thoroughly combine sour cream, cottage cheese,
salt, onion and garlic.
Gently fold in potatoes.
Pour into prepared casserole dish.
Sprinkle evenly with cheese and lightly sprinkle with paprika.
Bake at 350 degrees until heated through and lightly
browned, 40-45 minutes.

SERVES: 4

FATS PER SERVING: FAT FREE

Notes: _____

_____

_____

_____

Rating For This Recipe	
❏ Poor	❏ Fair
❏ Good	❏ Excellent

SUNKISSED CARROTS

1 pound carrots, peeled and sliced
1 teaspoon dried minced onions
Dash of garlic salt
Dash of pepper
1 tablespoon brown sugar substitute
1 cup of pineapple-orange-flavored diet soda.

METHOD:
Boil carrots until tender.
Drain well.
Add onions, garlic salt, pepper, brown sugar plus
1 cup pineapple-orange soda.
Mix well.
Simmer on low heat about 10 minutes.

SERVES: 4

FATS PER SERVING: FAT FREE

Rating For This Recipe
❏ Poor ❏ Fair
❏ Good ❏ Excellent

Notes: _____
_____
_____
_____

TOMATO SAUCE ITALIAN STYLE

1 can prepared tomato sauce
1 teaspoon oregano
1 clove crushed fresh garlic
1 teaspoon sweet basil
1 onion (chopped)
1/4 teaspoon pepper
1 chicken-flavored bouillon cube (crushed)

METHOD:
Add all of the above ingredients
in a small saucepan and simmer for 15 minutes,
stirring occasionally.
Can be used as a sauce for eggplant, spaghetti,
macaroni, or pizza.

SERVES: 4

FATS PER SERVING: FAT FREE

Notes: _____

_____

_____

_____

Rating For This Recipe
❏ Poor ❏ Fair
❏ Good ❏ Excellent

TOMATO BAKE

6 or 8 peeled and cut up tomatoes
1 teaspoon salt
1/2 teaspoon cloves
1 bay leaf
1/8 teaspoon pepper
1 medium onion, chopped fine

METHOD:
Sauté onion in a pan sprayed with non-stick cooking spray.
Add other ingredients and cook over a low heat
for 30 minutes.
Remove bay leaf.
Preheat oven to 350 degrees.
Mix above ingredients with 6 slices FAT FREE bread
that has been torn in small pieces.
Place in baking dish and bake for I hour.

SERVES: 4-6

FATS PER SERVING: FAT FREE

Rating For This Recipe
❑ Poor ❑ Fair
❑ Good ❑ Excellent

Notes: _____

_____

_____

_____

YUMMY GRILLED POTATOES

1 large baking potato for each serving
1 medium onion for each serving, sliced
1/3 teaspoon chives per serving
Salt and pepper to taste

METHOD:
Scrub potatoes thoroughly.
Tear a piece of heavy-duty foil large enough to wrap
vegetables and allow for a double fold.
Spray wlth butter-flavored cooking spray.
Slice potato, top with sliced onion, salt and pepper and
chives.
Spray all with butter-flavored cooking spray.
Fold and seal foil tightly.
Grill over medium coals for about 30 minutes, turning often
to ensure even cooking.
May add FAT FREE margarine to packet when served.

FATS PER SERVING: FAT FREE

Notes: _____

_____

_____

_____

Rating For This Recipe	
❏ Poor	❏ Fair
❏ Good	❏ Excellent

ZIPPY POTATOES

Preheat over to 375 degrees

6 large baking potatoes
1 cup shredded FAT FREE sharp Cheddar cheese
1/2 cup tomato juice
1/3 cup FAT FREE sour cream
Paprika
Salt and pepper to taste

METHOD:
Scrub potatoes.
Spray with non-stick butter-flavored cooking spray
and prick with fork.
Bake 1 hour and 15 minutes, or until tender.
Remove from oven and increase temperature to 400 degrees.
Slice each potato in half lengthwise, scoop out inside
leaving a thick shell.
In a large mixing bowl, mash potatoes, mixing in cheese,
tomato juice, salt and pepper to taste and the
FAT FREE sour cream.
Sprinkle paprika on each potato half after filling shell
with mashed potato mixture.
Return to oven and bake 15-20 minutes or until tops are
lightly browned.
Can be prepared ahead and frozen.
If frozen, bake for 25 minutes at 350 degrees.

SERVING: 6

FATS PER SERVING: TRACE

Rating For This Recipe
❏ Poor ❏ Fair
❏ Good ❏ Excellent

Notes: _____
_____
_____
_____

ZUCCHINI SAUTÉ

3 medium zucchini, thinly sliced
1 small green pepper, coarsely chopped
2 cloves garlic, minced
1 cup fresh sliced mushrooms
1/8 teaspoon black pepper
1 tablespoon FAT FREE famous brand margarine

METHOD:
Heat skillet. Remove from stove and with nozzle
facing away from stove, spray skillet with butter-flavored
cooking spray.
Replace on heat and add vegetables and pepper.
Stir and sauté over medium heat until tender.
Remove from heat and stir in FAT FREE margarine.
Toss to coat vegetables.
Serve immediately

SERVES: 6-8

FATS PER SERVING: FAT FREE

Notes: _____

_____

_____

_____

Rating For This Recipe
❑ Poor ❑ Fair
❑ Good ❑ Excellent

SECTION THREE

Planning your own 28-day menu

-how we do it at the LowFat Connection
-AND how you can do it too
-things to know about menu planning

By now you are chomping at the bit to get started on your own low-fat menu planning. We want to help.

You'll see an outline for a 7-day menu plan. This is built around the same format that we use at the LowFat Connection.

You'll enjoy working through the recipes in this book and then building your own meals.**

I've also included a sample first page to give you an idea how we do it at LFC.

Of course, you can do what is best for your own tastes.

Caution: Be careful when you are planning your desserts. That can really get you into big trouble real fast.

** Or you can join the LFC team. Our BASIC PLAN consists of the 28-day planned menu, a monthly newsletter and local support group meetings whenever possible.

Others of you may want our BASIC DELUXE planned menu which is a tailor-made menu for your eating-out places.

For more information contact us at:

LowFat Connection
1401 Professional Blvd.
Evansville, Indiana 47715

812-473-1052

Or call our toll free order line at:

1-800-343-8101

In the following pages, you'll see how we actually do it at LFC. I've provided you with a sample "day one" page from one of our menus we've used before. Notice it has a portion size, ingredient (food name) and fat gram count section. These fall under meal types: breakfast, lunch, dinner and so forth.

Based upon your reading thus far and the recipes in this book, you can now actually start your own menu.

Again, consulting a physician before starting any kind of "diet" plan is useful and needed.

Remember, there is power in writing things down!

When I lost my 110 pounds almost eight years ago, I never went to bed at night without WRITING DOWN what I was going to eat the next day.

Professionals know the power of the written word.

And you can too. You'll be amazed with how it works.

It's time to go to work.

It all started 7 seven years ago . . .

YOUR OWN SAMPLE PLAN

BASIC MEAL PLAN: DAY 1   THE LOW FAT CONNECTION

Portion Size   Food Names   Fat Grams
**************   ***************   ***********

BREAKFAST

_____   _____   _____
_____   _____   _____
_____   _____   _____
_____   _____   _____

SNACK

_____   _____   _____
_____   _____   _____
_____   _____   _____

LUNCH

_____   _____   _____
_____   _____   _____
_____   _____   _____
_____   _____   _____

DINNER

_____   _____   _____
_____   _____   _____
_____   _____   _____
_____   _____   _____

SNACK

_____   _____   _____
_____   _____   _____
_____   _____   _____

FAT GRAMS: _____

BASIC MEAL PLAN: DAY 2   THE LOW FAT CONNECTION

| Portion Size | Food Names | Fat Grams |
| *************** | *************** | ************ |

BREAKFAST

———————   ————————————   ————————
———————   ————————————   ————————
———————   ————————————   ————————
———————   ————————————   ————————

SNACK

———————   ————————————   ————————
———————   ————————————   ————————
———————   ————————————   ————————

LUNCH

———————   ————————————   ————————
———————   ————————————   ————————
———————   ————————————   ————————
———————   ————————————   ————————

DINNER

———————   ————————————   ————————
———————   ————————————   ————————
———————   ————————————   ————————
———————   ————————————   ————————

SNACK

———————   ————————————   ————————
———————   ————————————   ————————
———————   ————————————   ————————

FAT GRAMS: _____

BASIC MEAL PLAN: DAY 3 THE LOW FAT CONNECTION

| Portion Size | Food Names | Fat Grams |
| ************** | **************** | ************ |

BREAKFAST

————	————————	————
————	————————	————
————	————————	————
————	————————	————

SNACK

————	————————	————
————	————————	————
————	————————	————

LUNCH

————	————————	————
————	————————	————
————	————————	————
————	————————	————

DINNER

————	————————	————
————	————————	————
————	————————	————
————	————————	————

SNACK

————	————————	————
————	————————	————
————	————————	————

FAT GRAMS: _____

BASIC MEAL PLAN: DAY 4   THE LOW FAT CONNECTION

| Portion Size | Food Names | Fat Grams |
| ************* | *************** | ************ |

BREAKFAST

_____   _____   _____

_____   _____   _____

_____   _____   _____

_____   _____   _____

SNACK

_____   _____   _____

_____   _____   _____

_____   _____   _____

LUNCH

_____   _____   _____

_____   _____   _____

_____   _____   _____

_____   _____   _____

DINNER

_____   _____   _____

_____   _____   _____

_____   _____   _____

_____   _____   _____

SNACK

_____   _____   _____

_____   _____   _____

_____   _____   _____

FAT GRAMS: _____

BASIC MEAL PLAN: DAY 5   THE LOW FAT CONNECTION

Portion Size   Food Names   Fat Grams
*************   ***************   ************

BREAKFAST

_____   _____   _____
_____   _____   _____
_____   _____   _____
_____   _____   _____

SNACK

_____   _____   _____
_____   _____   _____
_____   _____   _____

LUNCH

_____   _____   _____
_____   _____   _____
_____   _____   _____
_____   _____   _____

DINNER

_____   _____   _____
_____   _____   _____
_____   _____   _____
_____   _____   _____

SNACK

_____   _____   _____
_____   _____   _____
_____   _____   _____

FAT GRAMS: _____

BASIC MEAL PLAN: DAY 6   THE LOW FAT CONNECTION

Portion Size   Food Names   Fat Grams
***************   ***************   ************

BREAKFAST

_____   _____   _____
_____   _____   _____
_____   _____   _____
_____   _____   _____

SNACK

_____   _____   _____
_____   _____   _____
_____   _____   _____

LUNCH

_____   _____   _____
_____   _____   _____
_____   _____   _____
_____   _____   _____

DINNER

_____   _____   _____
_____   _____   _____
_____   _____   _____
_____   _____   _____

SNACK

_____   _____   _____
_____   _____   _____
_____   _____   _____

FAT GRAMS: _____

BASIC MEAL PLAN: DAY 7   THE LOW FAT CONNECTION

Portion Size   Food Names   Fat Grams
**************   ***************   ************

BREAKFAST

_____   _____   _____
_____   _____   _____
_____   _____   _____
_____   _____   _____

SNACK

_____   _____   _____
_____   _____   _____
_____   _____   _____

LUNCH

_____   _____   _____
_____   _____   _____
_____   _____   _____
_____   _____   _____

DINNER

_____   _____   _____
_____   _____   _____
_____   _____   _____
_____   _____   _____

SNACK

_____   _____   _____
_____   _____   _____
_____   _____   _____

FAT GRAMS: _____

Meal Plan Name: BDAY1   THE LOW FAT CONNECTION

Portion Size	Food Names	FAT GRAMS
*************	***************	**************
	BREAKFAST	0
	Applesauce canned no sugar	0
	Banana	0
1 pkg. instant	Oatmeal hot cereal w/o salt	2*
	ANY FAT FREE BREAD	0
	SNACK	0
	Any Fruit, Your Choice	0
	LUNCH	0
3 Ounce(s)	Turkey	3*
	ANY FAT FREE BREAD	0
	Mayonnaise, Fat Free	0
	Applesauce canned no sugar	0
	DINNER	0
2 Cup(s)	Pasta spaghetti cooked	2*
1 Cup(s)	Spaghetti Sauce-Chunky	8*
1 Piece(s)	ITALIAN BREADSTICK	2*
	GARDEN SALAD/FAT FREE DRESSING	0
	SNACK	0
1 Packet	1/2 BAG POPCORN	4*

FAT GRAMS: 21

* Fat gram count is based on controlled serving sizes.
(Also, it should be noted that high calorie sweets and desserts should be limited, even if they are fat free. These are the "bad" kind of calories that will cause weight gain.)

FAST FOOD ALTERNATIVES

Fast food is a tricky business for the one concerned with weight loss.

My husband and I had no idea just how tricky it could really be. Oh, we knew that it could really throw you off in a weight-loss program, but, we had no idea until we started looking into the fat grams of these fast-food meals. So, what we found out was that when you looked at these menus from a fat gram count point of view, there was very little awareness for the consumer.

She might have seen something on television or heard something at work. Still, she has little information to work with once inside the fast-food place. My husband and I went through one menu offered by a national chain restaurant and about 85% of the menu offerings were unacceptable by fat gram standards. That's not to say that you can't "rob Peter to pay Paul" because we teach this principle, but you must know how to do it.

Another thing, if you do not know what you're going to eat BEFORE you go into the fast-food place or drive up to the drive-up window, you're not likely to follow through properly. In order to counteract this problem and to give our readers an advantage, we include the following "Fast Food Alternatives" listing for your convenience.

Many of our people at LFC carry a fat gram counter book with them at all times. That's fine. It works. But, if you can't do that, plan ahead and use our listing as a resource.

The following places are listed in alphabetical order and you will notice that we have the food portions to the left and the fat gram counts on the right column. Browse through them and increase your fat gram awareness.

FAST FOOD ALTERNATIVES

ARBY'S   FAT GRAMS

Chef Salad 10
Garden salad 5
Hot ham 'n cheese 14
Lite roast beef deluxe 10
Lite roast chicken deluxe 6
Roast beef junior 11
Roast chicken salad 7
Side Salad 0

BURGER KING   FAT GRAMS

Cheeseburger 15
Chicken tenders 13
Hamburger 11
Salad, chef... 9
Salad, garden 5
Salad, side 0

CHICK-FIL-A   FAT GRAMS

Carrot-Raisin salad 5
Chargrilled Chicken.......................................2
Chargrilled Chicken Deluxe Sandwich 5
Chargrilled Chicken Garden salad 2
Chick-Fil-A Sandwich 9
Chick-Fil-Q Sandwich 7
Tossed Salad w/ Lite Italian............................2
Ice dream 5
Lemon Pie.. 5

DAIRY QUEEN   FAT GRAMS

BBQ beef sandwich 4
Banana split..11
Cone regular.. 7
DQ sandwich 4
Float 7
Hamburger (Dairy Queen) 13
Malt reg. vanilla 14
Side salad no dressing 0

Strawberry shortcake 11
Strawberry waffle cn 12
Sundae Strawberry Yogurt 0
Sundae regular 8
Yogurt -reg cone 0

DOMINO'S PIZZA   FAT GRAMS

Pizza 14" PLAIN CHEESE 10
Pizza -3 slices Vegetable 10

HARDEE'S   FAT GRAMS

Apple turnover 12
Big roast beef 11
Chicken pasta salad 3
Chicken stix 6 pcs 9
Cinnamon/raisin biscuit 5
Fried egg... 6
Grilled chicken Sandwich 13
Grilled chicken 9
Hamburger 10
Pancakes (3) 2
Pancakes w/ 2 bacn 9
Roast Beef, Regular 9
Side salad 0

KENTUCKY FRIED CHICKEN   FAT GRAMS

Baked beans... 1
Chkn drum lite crsp 1
Chkn drum original 9
Chkn littles sandwich 10
Chkn side brst lite 12
Chkn wing original... 12
Cole slaw 6
Corn on the cob 3
Kentucky nuggets 3
Potato salad 9
Potatoes mash/gravy 1

LONG JOHN SILVER'S   FAT GRAMS

Baked 3pc (fish lemon) 1
Baked 3pc (fish paprika) 1

Baked 3pc (fish scampi) 5
Chicken light herb 4
Chicken plank 6
Clams breaded 12
Fish batter fried 8
Fries 10
Hushpuppies.. 4
Pie lemon meringue 7
Salad, ocean chef 9
Salad, seafood 6
Shrimp batter fried 3

MCDONALD'S   FAT GRAMS

Chicken Fajita (McDonald's) 8
Cookies McDonaldland 9
Egg McMuffin..11
Eggs scrambled.. 9
English muffin/butter 5
Frozen yogurt cone 1
Hamburger 10
Hash brown 7
Hotcakes w/btr,syrp 9
Ice cream cone 5
McLean deluxe w/o cheese 10
Muffin, Apple Bran (McDonald's)...........................0
Salad chunky chicken 3
Salad garden 7
Salad shrimp 3
Shake low fat choc 2
Shake low fat straw 1
Shake low fat van 1
Strawberry Sundae Yogurt...................................1
Sundae low fat carml 3
Sundae low fat ht fd 3
Sundae low fat straw 3

TACO BELL   FAT GRAMS

Chicken burrito 12
Cinnamon twists 8
Fajita steak taco 11
Fiesta burrito 9
Fiesta soft shell 7
Fiesta taco 7
Pepper's jalapeno 0
Pintos 'n cheese 9
Taco hard shell 11
Taco soft 12
Taco supreme 15
Tostada 11

WENDY'S   FAT GRAMS

Bread Stick 1
Chef salad 5
Chicken breast fillet 10
Chili 7
Garden salad 2
Grilled chicken sandwich 13
Jr. hamburger 9
Potato plain 0

-a word about vacations

FRANK'S SIDE

This year (1994) when we went on vacation in June, I was determined to change my vacation eating style. Every year it seems that I could count on gaining about 6-8 pounds on an 8-12 day vacation.

A couple of years ago when I went to Branson for three days, I gained 3 1/2 pounds! That's eating a great deal of food obviously. And the next year afterwards, we took a vacation to the Dakotas and Wyoming and Yellowstone for eleven days. I gained 8 1/2 pounds then.

How could I change this kind of an outcome on vacations?

So, this year I was thinking what I could do. We would be gone for 8 days on our "New England" tour including Quebec, Canada.

I meant for this to be in part a "business" trip for this experiment. Then I could report back to you the readers and to our LowFat Connection clients.

I'm happy to report that I gained only ONE POUND out of the trip.

Fantastic.

What did I do that was different from the other vacations?

First, I had a new way of thinking about eating on vacations. Usually I thought of vacation as the time when I pulled all the stops out and eat like a pig. That type of thinking changed. I would think differently this time. I did not want to have to pay the price of taking the weight back off. Each year it seemed to get harder and longer in taking the pounds off.

Secondly, I would eat sensibly. I knew there would be times when I would "pig out". But I would pace myself and not throw away my original game plan. It worked out great. I usually ate at

McDonald's and had my breakfast pancakes and a muffin, fat free. Or, if we were somewhere else, I would have oatmeal for breakfast. I stayed away from all the oils I could, and I made sure I had a "lite" salad dressing. Also, I bought myself a bottle of Molly McButter and used that for my baked potato seasoning. Most of the time, I found little alternatives for sour cream and butter.

Thirdly, I became more and more aware that most eating places are not "fat-buster" friendly.

You have to watch and be on guard constantly. I'm living proof you can eat sensibly on vacation and still have a great time!

Conclusion

The "fat-busting" bus has arrived at your doorstep. The task is now up to you.

Choices are important.

They empower you for a higher quality of life.

To lose 110 pounds and keep it off after seven, almost eight, years now is truly a "road less travelled". I'm amazed at just how simple these concepts are for success. Yet, they are very hard ones to implement because of all the excess baggage we carry:

Baggage contributed by the times in which we live.

Baggage contributed by where we are emotionally and psychologically and, yes, even spiritually.

That kind of baggage does not "have to" be carried once we're made aware of it. It can be cast off.

You can empower yourself by the choices you make.

Do you want to be thinner for life?

No doubt you are reading this book out of some interest for yourself or maybe you have some "significant other" in your life that prompts your reading, or some other reason.

Whatever the reason, you have a stake in the low-fat concepts presented.

Take these recipes and the information therein and personalize them for yourself. The material is not "set in stone". We offer only suggestions.

We seek progress, not perfection. This is how I have done it for myself.

"Attitude determines altitude" is not just verbal verbiage.

There's truth in that thought.

"Seek and ye shall find," is another truth-statement.

But what kind of seekers are we? are you?

Take your past experiences in weight loss, even your failures because I had them too, and see past them to learn from them, and get on with your life. Decide upon your own plan. Shape it to fit your own life and needs. Make your own reasonable goals.

I once read somewhere of the idea that there is no magic to lifetime, permanent weight loss. That is so true and clear. There is no "magic" to it, if by that you mean there's not any hard work involved. It DOES **We Hit the Mark!** take a lot of hard work and a constant watching. But I personally think it is worth it!

Finally, we look forward to meeting you in person somewhere, someplace. We challenge you to a "fatbusting" way of life.

s/Natoma Riley
July 23, 1994
Evansville, Indiana

JOIN . . .
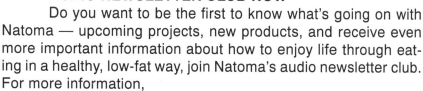

NATOMA RILEY'S
AUDIO NEWSLETTER CLUB NOW

Do you want to be the first to know what's going on with Natoma — upcoming projects, new products, and receive even more important information about how to enjoy life through eating in a healthy, low-fat way, join Natoma's audio newsletter club. For more information,

call toll-free order line 1-800-343-8101
OR write to: LFC
1401 Professional Blvd.
Evansville, IN 47715
812-473-1052

A Postscript

Deadlines are always a pain.

As we went to press, printers have deadlines as well.

My husband and I had committed to a recipe count for this book of some 200 plus. After considerable time and culling out duplicate recipes, we came up with a count of 192 at the deadline for printing.

But there is a thing called a "postscript" to a book. So, we give you a book of "200 plus recipes," thanks to this handy device.

Here are some extra recipes that you can enjoy.

TEXAS CASSEROLE

2 3-ounce LEAN pork chops OR
2 3-ounce chicken breasts
1 can famous brand cream of mushroom soup
1 cup uncooked rice
1 cup water
1/3 cup diced green onion
1/3 cup diced onion

METHOD:
In casserole mix rice, water and onions
Place meat on top
Cover with 1 can cream of mushroom soup.
Bake 1 hour uncovered at 350 degrees.

SERVES: 2

FATS PER SERVING: 5

CLAM DIP

8 ounces FAT FREE cream cheese
16 ounces FAT FREE sour cream
8 ounces FAT FREE mayonnaise
1 envelope famous brand name vegetable
soup and dip mix
6 green onions - chopped
1 can water chestnuts; drain and chop
1 can minced clams, rinsed and drained

METHOD:
Blend together, cream cheese, sour cream
and mayonnaise until smooth.
Stir in remaining ingredients and chill.
Serve with FAT FREE crackers.

FATS PER SERVING: FAT FREE

BROCCOLI LETTUCE SALAD

1 small bag of salad, or 1 head of lettuce
1 head of cauliflower
1 head of broccoli
1/2 cup red onion chopped
3/4 to 1 cup FAT FREE mayonnaise
1/3 cup FAT FREE Parmesan cheese
1/3 cup imitation bacon bits

METHOD:
Chop cauliflower and broccoli into small flowerets
Chop lettuce into smaller pieces too.
Mix thoroughly chilland enjoy

SERVES: 8

FATS PER SERVING: TRACE

BAKED CORN

Preheat oven to 350 degrees.

1 17-ounce can each of yellow cream-style corn
and whole kernel corn, drained (NOTE: Make sure
nutritional label reads TOTAL FATS: 0)
2 tablespoons sugar
1/2 cup each onion and bell pepper, chopped
2 pimientos, chopped
1 cup FAT FREE sharp Cheddar cheese, grated
1 cup cracker crumbs, FAT FREE
4 ounces egg substitute
2/3 cup skim milk
1/4 cup FAT FREE margarine, melted

METHOD:
Mix egg substitute with the milk and beat well.
Mix all ingredients in a 9 x 12 x 2-inch cake pan
or Pyrex dish.
Bake in oven for 1 hour

SERVES: 4

FATS PER SERVING: FAT FREE

EMERALD RICE

1 onion, chopped
10 ounces chopped, cooked broccoli
1 cup FAT FREE Cheddar cheese
2 cups cooked rice
1 10-1/4-ounce can cream of mushroom soup

METHOD:
In skillet, sauté chopped onion in
FAT FREE margarine.
Add cooked broccoli.
Add cooked rice; stir in mushroom soup.
Spray a casserole dish, put ingredients in dish.
Top with 1 cup grated FAT FREE cheddar cheese.
Bake at 350 degrees for 30 minutes.

SERVES: 6

FATS PER SERVING: 3

SQUASH CASSEROLE

4 ounces egg substitute
1/2 onion, chopped
1 10-3/4-ounce can cream of mushroom soup
1/2 cup FAT FREE margarine
1/2 cup FAT FREE buttered bread crumbs
2 cups cooked squash, well-drained
Season with dash of salt

METHOD:
Combine all ingredients except bread crumbs.
Pour in sprayed casserole and top with bread crumbs.
Bake in 350-degree oven for 30 minutes or
until hot and bubbly.
SERVES: 6

FATS PER SERVING: 3

LEMON BASIL CARROTS

1 pound baby carrots or medium carrots cut in 2 12-inch pieces
2 tablespoons FAT FREE margarine
1 tablespoon lemon juice
1/2 teaspoon garlic salt
1/2 teaspoon dried basil
Crunched dash of pepper

METHOD:
In saucepan, cook carrots in boiling water
for 20 to 30 minutes or until tender; drain.
In saucepan, melt margarine, stir in lemon juice,
salt, basil and then add carrots. Toss.
SERVES: 4-6

FATS PER SERVING: FAT FREE

CUCUMBER CASSEROLE

1 pound ground turkey breast
6 medium cucumbers
1 large onion, chopped
1 large bell pepper, chopped
2 cups celery, chopped
FAT FREE bread crumbs

METHOD:
Peel cucumbers and cut into small pieces.
Boil until tender, drain, put aside.
Brown meat. When brown, add onions, bell pepper
and celery and simmer for about 30 minutes.
Drain.
Add cucumbers to meat mixture and let
simmer for 25 to 30 minutes.
Pour into casserole.
If it is too thin, add bread crumbs to mixture.
(Put bread crumbs on top).
Bake in preheated oven at 325 degrees
for about 25 to 30 minutes.

SERVES: 6

FATS PER SERVING: 2

CABBAGE ROLLS

1 pound ground turkey breast
1 can tomatoes with green peppers and onions
1 cup rice, raw
Salt and pepper to taste

METHOD:
Mix all ingredients in a large bowl and put aside.
Meanwhile, take 1 head of cabbage in a
large pot of boiling water.
Put a large fork in center and place in the water
until it is tender.
Use knife and cut outside leaves off and cool them
slightly.
Put some mixture in center of leaf and roll it up
tight and secure with a toothpick.
Place the rolls in a pot just as tight fitting as you
can.
Then add water to cover the rolls. Use the same
water for boiling the cabbage.
Cook on medium heat until water is gone,
about 35 to 45 minutes.
Cabbage rolls can be stacked if your pot is too
small.

SERVES: 6

FATS PER SERVING: 2

SPAGHETTI PIE

1 pound ground turkey breast
6 ounces spaghetti
2 tablespoons FAT FREE margarine
1/3 cup grated FAT FREE Parmesan cheese
3 ounces egg substitute
1 cup cottage cheese (8 ounces)
1/2 cup chopped onion
1/4 cup green pepper, chopped
1 8-ounce can tomatoes (1 cup) cut up
1 6-ounce can tomato paste
1 teaspoon sugar
1 teaspoon dried oregano, crushed
1/2 teaspoon garlic salt
1/2 cup FAT FREE shredded Mozzarella cheese
(2 ounces)

METHOD:
Cook the spaghetti according to directions on package;
drain (should have about 3 cups spaghetti).
Stir margarine into hot spaghetti.
Stir Parmesan cheese and form spaghetti mixture into a
"crust" in a sprayed 10-inch plate.
Spread cottage cheese over bottom of spaghetti crust.
In a skillet, cook ground meat, onion, green pepper until
vegetables are tender and meat is brown.
Drain off excess fat.
Stir in undrained tomatoes, tomato paste, sugar,
oregano and garlic salt; heat through.
Turn meat mixture into spaghetti crust.
Bake, uncovered, in a 350-degree oven for 20 minutes.
Sprinkle the Mozzarella cheese on top.
Bake 5 minutes longer or until cheese melts.

SERVINGS: 6

FATS PER SERVING: 2

INDEX